WICKED
CONDUCT

DATE DUE

WICKED CONDUCT

The Minister, the Mill Girl and the Murder that Captivated Old Rhode Island

RORY RAVEN

Charleston · London

THE
History
PRESS

Published by The History Press
Charleston, SC 29403
www.historypress.net

Copyright © 2009 by Rory Raven
All rights reserved

First published 2009

Manufactured in the United States

ISBN 978.1.59629.802.6

Library of Congress CIP data applied for.

Given the subject, it may seem strange to dedicate this book to my wife, Judith, but I think she'll understand.

Contents

ACKNOWLEDGEMENTS

No one writes a book on their own. The following were all of assistance in either tangible or ineffable ways:

As always, my wife Judith, who puts up with a lot; Neville Bedford and Daniel Ciora, my legal team; the staff of the Bristol and Tiverton Town Clerks' Offices, who exhibited a professionalism and helpfulness I have rarely experienced among municipal clerks; the staff of the Bristol Historical and Preservation Society; David Brussat, for fearlessly balancing on a recycling bin; Allison Bundy and Rosemary Cullen of Brown University, for putting up with endless "Oh, yeah, one more thing…" requests; Ken Carlson of the Rhode Island State Archives; Jen Coleman-Hall, for sorting out the vagaries of nineteenth-century female dress; Megan Delaney of the Newport Historical Society—if you need anything there, she's the one to talk to; Lawrence DePetrillo, who has a picture of everything; Betty Fitzgerald of the Providence Public Library; Jill Jann, for her patient encouragement; Dr. Omar Meer, for medical advice; Connie Mendes of the Fall River Historical Society; Deborah Newton, my personal cartographer, and Paul Di Filippo, just for being Paul Di Filippo; Dale Peterson of the United Methodist Archives, for help in image wrangling; the lovely Saunders Robinson at The History Press; Ian Rowland, an endless source of inspiration and encouragement; Will Schaff, for his help with images and for just being a good friend; Andy Smith of the Rhode Island Judicial Archives; Nancy Smith, Kennedy Park's manager/director, for showing me the scene of the crime; Elizabeth Wayland-Seal, for coming up with ninepence when I needed it; and to you, for being someone who reads thank-yous.

CHAPTER 1

"I Discovered Her to Be Dead"

Tiverton, Rhode Island, is a small town in an eastern corner of the state, looking out over the waters of Mount Hope Bay. In 1832, it was a rural village of some three thousand souls, mostly farmers raising cattle and working the thin, rocky New England soil. Its only claims to fame might have been the views offered from atop its rolling hills or that it sheltered refugees driven out of nearby Newport by the invading Redcoats in 1776.

The main road running north crossed the state line and led into the burgeoning factory town of Fall River, Massachusetts, loud with the sounds of industry. Mills identified Fall River in the same way that fields identified Tiverton.

John Durfee was a middle-aged Tiverton town councilman who also held the office of overseer of the poor. He lived on the family farm on the main road, half a mile from the Massachusetts border. He had no idea that he was about to make a macabre discovery that would catapult his sleepy little town into national headlines.

On the morning of Friday, December 21, 1832, Durfee opened the barn door and drove his small herd of cattle—his "creatures," as he called them—out into the cold. Yesterday had been milder, but today winter had returned, and his breath misted in the air and the "fog"—the dry, icy grass—snapped and crunched beneath his feet.

Looking out over the fields that sloped down to meet the bay, something strange caught his eye. There, in a stone-walled field enclosing a number

VIEW OF DURFEE'S FARM, WITH

Contemporary view of Durfee's stack yard, from Catherine Williams's *Fall River: An Authentic Narrative. Courtesy Brown University.*

E STACK YARD, &c. AT FALL-RIVER.

of haystacks, a heavy, dark shape moved slightly, swaying in the stiff breeze coming off the water.

Leaving his cattle for a moment, he went for a closer look.

There among the haystacks, hanging from a fence post, was the frozen body of a petite young woman, her disheveled dark hair hiding her face. Carefully parting the "frowzled" hair, Durfee discovered that she was a stranger. If he shivered, it wasn't just from the cold.

Her right cheek lay against the wooden stake from which she hung by the neck. Her eyes were closed and her tongue pushed slightly through her teeth. A bloody froth flecked her very red lips. Her legs were bent back under her, her knees within six inches of the ground, placing the body in a grotesque, almost kneeling position.

She wore a long cloak, fastened up nearly its entire length, save for the second or third hook down from the throat, and a calash—a kind of large, fancy bonnet. She was barefoot, her shoes placed carefully off to her right. On the ground to her left was a large red handkerchief or bandana. There was no sign of a struggle and, as he glanced around, no sign of anyone having been in the stack yard at all.

Durfee called out for help, and three men came running: his father, Richard Durfee, and two laborers from nearby farms.

"Cut her down," Richard Durfee commanded, and one laborer produced a knife. Cutting the cord a few inches from where it was tied around her neck, John Durfee and the others carefully laid the body down on the ground.

Durfee ran to summon Elihu Hicks, Tiverton's elderly coroner. By the time the old man reached the scene, word that a woman had hanged herself in Durfee's stack yard had spread up the road to Fall River, and a number of others had come to see for themselves, and a small and curious crowd had gathered.

Pushing through the little crowd, Hicks made a quick examination of the body. He noticed that the cord around the neck cut into the flesh and that, strangely, the ribbons of the calash were under the cord. Turning to those gathered, Hicks selected a jury of six men for an inquest on the body. Richard Durfee was elected foreman.

"Does anyone know her?" one of the men asked.

"She is well dressed," someone else said. "I think she must be someone respectable."

Among the crowd of onlookers were several who would play important roles as the story unfolded. A number of them remain indistinct figures—people who left behind little evidence and few records of their time here. Among

Haunting though inaccurate depiction of the discovery of Sarah's body from the 1870s pamphlet *The Terrible Hay Stack Murder*. Strangely, the captions are in both English and German. *Courtesy Brown University.*

these significant yet hazy figures is the Reverend Ira M. Bidwell. He seems to have been middle aged, married with children and at the time was the minister of Fall River's Methodist congregation.

"Yes, I know her," he said. "She is a respectable young woman, and a member of my church."

Arriving just behind Reverend Bidwell was Dr. Thomas Wilbur, a physician who likewise recognized the body. He knelt down by her, checking the cord and feeling her abdomen. The jury asked if he could identify her, and he said that she was Sarah Maria Cornell, a patient who had consulted him several times in recent weeks. Bidwell concurred that he knew her as Sarah Cornell.

The body was gently loaded onto a cart and brought to the Durfee house. Due to either the freezing weather or rigor mortis, the legs could not be straightened, and the body lay on its side. The men of the jury turned their attention to the cord around the neck. One who "had followed the sea" noted that it was tied in a clove hitch knot. A clove hitch is not a slip knot and "must be drawn at both ends horizontally to tighten it," the former sailor noted, tightened with both hands, making it a very odd—perhaps impossible—choice for a suicide. The cord was carefully cut and removed.

Because a group of men examining a woman's body would have been considered indecorous if not outright scandalous, several local women were called in and given the task of going over the body while the jury conferred in the next room. It is not clear why Dr. Wilbur did not take charge of the examination, but he seems to have been outside talking to Reverend Bidwell.

The women discovered that the right arm was bent up at the elbow, with the back of the hand nearly brushing up against the chin. Calling for warm water and hot cloths, they wrapped the arm and attempted to straighten it. It took considerable effort, but it finally moved with an audible snap. They must have thought they had broken the dead girl's arm.

Some noticed green grass stains and scratches on her knees. Worse, there were several bruises on the lower abdomen. One of the women, Dorcas Ford, said that "rash violence" seemed to have been done to the unfortunate corpse.

Outside, Durfee asked Reverend Bidwell if Sarah had any family or friends in the area who would take charge of her remains and make funeral arrangements. Perhaps speaking in his role as overseer of the poor, Durfee suggested that if such was not the case Bidwell himself could make the necessary arrangements, as she had been a member of his congregation.

Durfee's stack yard is now part of the northwest corner of Kennedy Park in Fall River, Massachusetts. *Photo by Robert O'Brien.*

Bidwell said he knew little of her and that she had been only a new arrival, was still on probation and was not a full member. He would, he said, make inquiries and get back to him with a decision.

Heading north into Fall River, Durfee went to Sarah's boardinghouse in search of more information about her and especially about whatever family she might have left behind, who would need to be notified. Upon reaching the house, the shocked landlady, Harriet Hathaway, told him that Sarah Cornell was her only boarder and had lived there for just three short weeks. She worked as a weaver in one of the many local cotton mills, with Harriet's daughter, Lucy. Sarah had come home early yesterday afternoon, had a quick supper and changed her clothes before heading out, saying she was going to "Joseph Durfee's" (everyone in the area seems to have been named Durfee or Borden), and that she would be back before nine o'clock. But Sarah never returned, and Harriet eventually went to bed around ten o'clock, leaving the door unlocked just in case.

Durfee asked to see her belongings, saying that he and the women needed something to lay her out in, and Harriet gave him a locked trunk and a bandbox from her room, commenting that Sarah usually kept the key to the trunk in her pocket. Bringing the trunk and bandbox—a kind of round box used to hold odds and ends—back to Tiverton, he had one of the women retrieve the key from Sarah's pocket. In the trunk, among her clothes and other items, were several letters.

One on pink paper, addressed "Miss Sarah M. Connell, Fall River, Mass. To be left at Mrs. Cole's," ran as follows:

Providence Nov 1831

Dear Sister—I received your letter in due season and should have answered it before now but thought I would wait till this opportunity—as I told you I am willing to help you and do for you as circumstances are I should rather you would come to this place, viz. Bristol in the stage the 18th December and stop at the Hotel and stay till 6 in the evening and then go up directly across the main street to a brick building neare to the stone meeting house where I will meet you and talk with you when you stop at the tavern either inquire for work or go out on to the street in pretence of looking for some or something else and I may see you say nothing about me or my family should it storm on the 18th come the 20th—if you cannot come and it will be more convenient to meet me at the Methodist meeting house in Summerset just over the ferry on either of the above eve'g I will meet you there at the same hour or if you cannot do either I will come to Fall River on one of the above evenings back of the same meeting house where I once saw you at any hour you say on either of the above evenings when there will be the least passing I should think before the mills stop work this I will leave with you if I come I will come if it does not storm very hard if it does the first I'll come the second write me soon and tell me which—when you write direct your letter to Betsey Hills Bristol and not as you have to me remember this your last letter I am afraid was broken open

Were [wear] your callash and not your plain bonnet you can send your letter by mail. Yours, &c. B.H.

S.M.C.

let me still enjoin the secret keep the letters in your bosom or burn them up

Another, on pale yellow or "straw" colored paper, was likewise addressed to "Miss Sarah M. Connell Fall River Mass."

Nov 13, 1832

I have just received your letter with no small supprize and will say I will do all you ask only keep your secret—I wish you to write me as soon as you get this nameing some time and place where I shall see you and then look for answer before I come and will say wether convenient or not

Nº 3.

Nov 13th 1832

I have just Received your letter with no small supprise and will say I will do all you ask only keep your secrets ___ I wish you to write me as soon as you get this nameing some time and place where I shall see you and then look for answer before I come and will say whether convenient or not and will say the time — I will keep your letter till I see you and wish you to keep mine and have them at the time write soon say nothing to no one

Yours in haste

Reproduction of the yellow letter; the original letters are long lost, but an enterprising publisher released "A Facsimile of the Letters Produced at the Trial of the Reverend Ephraim K. Avery, on an Indictment for the Murder of Sarah Maria Cornell." *Courtesy Brown University.*

and will say the time. I will keep your letter till I see you and wish you to keep mine and have them at the time write soon say nothing to no one Yours in haste.

The third had the appearance of a hastily scribbled note, written on half a sheet of white paper:

Fall River, Dec 8
I will be here on the 20th if pleasant at the place named at 6 o'clock if not pleasant the next Monday eve.—say nothing.

The last one, undated and still sealed, was addressed to Reverend Bidwell:

Fall River
Rev. Mr. Bidwell
Sir—I take this opportunity to inform you that for reasons known to God and my own soul I wish no longer to be connected with the Methodist

Facsimile of Sarah's letter to Bidwell. *Courtesy Brown University.*

society —when I came to this place I thought I should enjoy myself among them but as I do not enjoy any religion at all I have not seen a well or happy day since I left Thompson Camp-meeting ground, you will therefore please to drop my name from Mr. Greene's class and I will try to gain all the instruction I can from your publick labours I hope I shall feel different some time or other—The Methodists are my people when I enjoy any religion—To them I was indebted under God for my spiritual

birth—I once knew what it was to love God with all my heart and felt that God was my father Jesus my friend and Heaven my home but have awfully departed—and sometimes fear I shall lose my soul forever I desire your prayers that God would keep me from this—
Yours respectfully Sarah M. Cornell—

The next day, Saturday, December 22, Durfee delivered these letters to Elihu Hicks, who submitted them to the jury.

Now the story began to take shape in their minds: Sarah had been involved with a man. Apparently, it was an illicit relationship, as the letters indicated a good deal of secrecy.

Dr. Wilbur, a plainspoken Quaker, told the jury what he knew of Sarah Cornell. Like Harriet Hathaway, he also knew her as a mill girl who worked as a weaver in a Fall River factory. She had consulted him in his Fall River office about eight weeks ago to determine if she was pregnant. After examining her, he concluded that she was in fact with child. Sarah took the news poorly; she was unmarried and alone, with no friends or family in the area. When Wilbur quietly asked who the father was, she named Ephraim K. Avery, a married Methodist minister across the bay in Bristol, Rhode Island.

Over the course of half a dozen visits, Wilbur's role seems to have changed from physician to advisor, as Sarah asked for his opinion about what to do. When he suggested she expose him—part punishment, part public service—Sarah shook her head gravely and refused.

"I cannot consent to bring such disgrace and trouble upon the church, and upon his innocent family, too," she said. "He has a worthy woman for a wife, and she and all his innocent children must be disgraced if he is exposed."

He suggested that she insist Avery support her and her child, but she again refused, saying, "The Methodist ministers are poor—all poor. They are very illy paid for their services, and I doubt his power to make up such a sum, besides I should not dare to name so much for fear he would think I had told some one."

One night, coming to Wilbur's office directly after work, she said that she had seen Avery when he had been in Fall River, preaching. Stepping out of the hearing of the others gathered there, she and Avery spoke quietly and he recommended she take thirty to forty drops of oil of tansy. Tansy is a flowering herb that, in small doses, has a variety of medicinal uses; since the Middle Ages, however, it has been taken in large doses to induce abortion.

Wilbur was shocked and warned her to do no such thing. Oil of tansy should only be used under a doctor's close supervision, and four to five drops was the usual amount prescribed. Such a large dose would probably induce abortion, but "it would endanger her life, or if she lived through it, would destroy her health."

"Then I will not take it," Sarah replied solemnly. "For I had rather have my child and do the best I can, than to endanger my life."

Wilbur added that, despite this, "she never did in my hearing express any but feelings of kindness and sympathy for him [Reverend Avery], and his family."

The coroner's jury reasoned that Sarah must have changed her mind, and in her despondency chose to end her life there in the stack yard. A tragic story, to be sure, but unfortunately not an unusual one. After some deliberation—with some raising the possibility of murder—the jury returned a verdict of suicide:

> *State of Rhode Island and Providence Plantations, Newport, ss. An Inquisition taken at Tiverton, in the County of Newport, the 21st day of December, 1832, before Elihu Hicks, coroner of the town of Tiverton, upon the view of the dead body of Sarah M. Cornell here lying dead, upon their oaths do say that the said Sarah was found dead hung up and confined, with a small cord or rope about her neck, to a stake inside of said stack yard, and the jurors do further say that they believe the said Sarah M. Cornell committed suicide by hanging herself upon a stake in said stack yard and was influenced to commit the crime by the wicked conduct of a married man, which we gather from Dr. Wilbour together with the contents of three letters found in the trunk of the said Sarah M. Cornell, and so the jurors aforesaid, &c. RICHARD DURFEE, Foreman, (et al).*

Bidwell soon asserted that Sarah Cornell was a "bad character," and as such his congregation would have nothing to do with her. No doubt puzzled by the minister's dramatic reversal—just yesterday he had deemed her "a respectable young woman and a member of my church"—Durfee took charge of the body and arranged to have it buried on his land. Reverend Fowler, a more liberal Congregationalist from Fall River, performed the funeral for a small group gathered on the Durfee farm.

Durfee probably thought that a long two days had come to an end and that the regrettable episode was over. And he may have wondered exactly who Sarah Maria Cornell had been.

CHAPTER 2

"The Narrative of This Unfortunate Female"

Sarah Maria Cornell was born on May 2, 1802, in Rupert, Vermont, the youngest of four children born into a failing marriage. Her mother, Lucretia Leffingwell, was from a well-off family of paper merchants in Norwich, Connecticut. Lucretia fell in love with James Cornell, an apprentice in one of her father's shops, and pursued the romance against her family's wishes. Eventually, the Leffingwell patriarch relented and the two were married. James Cornell moved his new bride to Vermont and proved himself to be a wastrel, content to borrow large sums from his father-in-law to support a growing family. After years of being regarded as an endless source of ready cash advances, Leffingwell refused to come across with another penny, and James Cornell promptly vanished from the scene, leaving his wife to care for their four children.

Lucretia moved the family back to Connecticut. Her father died in 1810, leaving her only a small portion of his estate. The children went into the care of various relatives with Sarah, usually called Maria by the family, going to an aunt. There seems to have been very little contact between some of them for years. Some accounts mention only three children, apparently losing track of the fourth altogether.

Sarah's early life is cloudy (which is not to say the rest of her life is exactly clear). At age fifteen, she went to work first for one local tailor (who may have fired her for being "negligent") and then shortly moved on to another, completing her apprenticeship in 1820 at age eighteen. She lived with her mother in Norwich, a city of about five thousand souls, and helped bring in some extra money with her needle. It wasn't easy. According to Gurdon Williams, a family friend and author of *Brief and Impartial Narrative of the Life of Sarah Maria Cornell*, Sarah's skills were "too imperfect" for her to set up a shop of her own. Even if she were more skilled than supposed, it would have been difficult for a young woman to set up her own shop, and there may not have been enough business to support the venture.

Williams described the teenaged Sarah:

> *Her personal appearance and address attractive—she was of middling stature, of dark complexion, with dark hazel eyes, and black hair—in her address and manners she was easy, unassuming and familiar perhaps to a fault—in her conversation she was intelligent, sprightly and interesting and in every respect admirably fitted to secure the esteem and friendship of her associates—but alas! With all these endowments, the poor misguided girl suffered herself too early to become the victim of contending passions. At age sixteen, she became extremely fond of dress, as well as of gay and lively company; and a fondness of visiting with her female companions scenes of innocent amusement and pleasure—her associates were respectable, but by indulging too frequently a fondness to enjoy their society, she became somewhat negligent of her needle.*

In 1822, her mother brought her to Providence to visit her older sister, also named Lucretia. With the family being split up after the death of James Cornell, Sarah had not seen Lucretia since they were very young children. "Oh shall I behold the face of my beloved sister which I have never seen or have no recollection of!" an excited Sarah wrote in a letter just before the visit.

Growing up in small Vermont and Connecticut towns, Sarah may have been overwhelmed making her way down the streets of a bustling city, the state capital, with a population of some sixteen thousand, with mills and hotels and immigrants from foreign ports of call. She would have been jostled by the busy populace, seen China trade clipper ships lying at anchor in the harbor and had merchants clamoring for her attention.

During her lengthy stay, Sarah got into trouble when she was accused of shoplifting a bonnet, a shawl and some lace at a dry goods store in the city's Cheapside section. She was caught and the unused items were tearfully returned. She ran further afoul of local merchants when she purchased a silk dress from another shop on credit and then failed to make payments. Sarah left Providence in disgrace and returned to Connecticut.

BRIEF AND IMPARTIAL NARRATIVE
OF THE
LIFE
OF
SARAH MARIA CORNELL,

Who was found dead (suspended by the neck and suspected to have been murdered) near Fall River, (Mass.) December 22, 1832.

WRITTEN BY ONE, WHO,
Early knew her—when her mind
" Untainted then by art,
Was noble, just, humane and kind
And virtue warm'd her heart—
——But, ah! the cruel spoiler came !"

NEW-YORK,
PRINTED FOR AND PUBLISHED BY G. WILLIAMS.

A portrait of Sarah adorns the cover of the 1833 pamphlet, *Brief and Impartial Narrative of the Life of Sarah Maria Cornell, Who Was Found Dead (Suspended by the Neck and Suspected to Have Been Murdered) Near Fall River (Mass.) December 22, 1832, Written by One Who Early Knew Her… Courtesy Brown University.*

One possible explanation for Sarah's behavior is that she and her sister had made the acquaintance of a young tailor by the name of Grindall Rawson, and they may have competed for his affections. Sarah may have sought to spruce up her rural wardrobe with a few items from the store, hoping to catch Rawson's eye, later making off with the dress for the same reason.

Whether this speculation is true or not, the two sisters did not speak to each other for some time after Sarah's departure from Providence, and Lucretia married Rawson some time later.

Cast adrift and living by herself, Sarah made a couple of significant changes. She abandoned her tailoring and took jobs in a string of local cotton mills, working as a weaver and operating the water-powered looms. The next few years of her life find her scraping along, moving from town to town, from mill to mill. The family did not approve.

New England mills of the time drew much of their labor force from young rural women. Life in the mills consisted of long hours—often sunrise to after sunset, six days a week—usually for very little pay. Some mills worked on the "Rhode Island system" and paid only in credit at stores and eateries owned by the same company that owned the mill itself. Many of the young women who entered millwork saw it as only a temporary measure to make a little bit of cash before being rescued from their toil by a dashing new husband. Mill owners did nothing to discourage their dreams, as it kept a steady stream of young women coming to their doors, seeking work.

A "mill girl" works a loom; Sarah performed a similar job in several mills throughout New England. *Courtesy Larry DePetrillo.*

About this time, Sarah also experienced a religious conversion. The Second Great Awakening was in full swing, with religious revivals sweeping through New England, kindling the fervor of many blue-collar Protestants. She flirted briefly with Congregationalism before being baptized into the Methodist Episcopal Church. She entered the church eagerly—perhaps too eagerly. According to Gurdon Williams, "There is a line where religion and piety terminates, and enthusiasm begins, and it is supposed that Maria overstepped this line and wandered away into the mazy and unexplored regions of religious fanaticism."

With her fondness for "dress, as well as of gay and lively company," it might be tempting to write Sarah off as simply a party girl, but letters she wrote in her twenties reveal a thoughtful, introspective side to her personality. The letters often contain Bible quotes and spiritual meditations. We can't be sure whether an introspective nature was sharpened by her conversion, or if the conversion gave rise to a period of self-reflection. But either way, Sarah shows herself to be contemplative and even eloquent.

In 1821, she wrote a letter to her sister noting that "the solemn bell has just summoned another fellow mortal into eternity." A neighboring family's servant, "a tall stout robust negro," had died unexpectedly after a brief illness. The nineteen-year-old Sarah pondered:

> *It is not for us to say whether he is happy or miserable in another world, but his death has very solemnly impressed my mind. Sometime I think* why am I spared *perhaps to commit more sin, perhaps for some usefulness. Sometimes I think I am no worse than others. What have I to fear, but God says be ye also ready for ye know not what hour the Lord will come.*

A Methodist camp meeting in the 1830s. Preachers on the stand at left exhort a large and enthusiastic crowd, with numerous white tents in the background. *Courtesy United Methodist Archives, Drew University.*

After a few more moves and brief stints working in various mill towns—Killingly, Dorchester, Taunton—Sarah settled in Lowell, Massachusetts, in May 1828. Lowell was a fast-growing industrial town, with six mills in operation, each employing well over a thousand workers, three more mills under construction and more on the drawing board. Over five million yards of cotton cloth rolled out of Lowell each year.

There was also a Methodist congregation there, and Sarah attended services and made a formal application for membership.

One month after her arrival, the congregation installed a new elder, the Reverend Ephraim Kingsbury Avery.

CHAPTER 3

"Such a Perfect Consciousness
of Innocency"

O n Friday, a few hours after viewing the body of the dead woman
and hearing what Dr. Wilbur had to say, Reverend Bidwell left
the stack yard and was on his way to Bristol, looking for his colleague
Reverend Avery.

Information about Ephraim Avery's background and early life is scanty. He
was born in December 1798 in either Connecticut or western Massachusetts
(sources disagree) and was the son of Lavinia and Amos Avery; his father
was a veteran of the Revolutionary War. Ephraim seems to have spent time
as a farmer and then a storekeeper and even briefly studied medicine before
joining the Methodist ministry in 1822.

Methodism traces its origins back to the theological teachings of brothers
John and Charles Wesley in eighteenth-century England. Derided by their
critics for their strict, "methodical" approach to religion, they preached
outdoors to the ordinary, workaday people who, they felt, had been ignored
and ill served by a haughty Church of England. From its early days,
Methodism had sought to bring its message of repentance and salvation
directly to the people, rather than expecting the people to seek out the
church. In America, as part of the Second Great Awakening, the movement
flourished, with numerous congregations (also called "meetings" or
"societies") being established. Each meeting was subdivided into "classes" of
about a dozen members. Acting as a kind of spiritual support group, classes
met weekly to pray and discuss their progress toward "Christian Perfection."
This setup may owe something to the Wesley brothers' own "Holy Club,"

REV. EPHRAIM K. AVERY.

[Drawn by a very celebrated Portrait Painter, and engraved by a first
rate Artist, and may be depended upon as a good Likeness.]

Portrait of Ephraim Avery. His supporters thought it was a good likeness, but detractors detected "a certain iron look, a pair of very thick lips, and a most unpleasant stare of the eyes." *Courtesy Brown University.*

the small group that met once a week in Oxford starting in 1792, giving rise to Methodism. The church was also very accepting of women, who were found in some lay roles of authority, such as class leaders.

Sarah Cornell, a woman from an undistinguished background working in a mill, was squarely in Methodism's target audience.

Methodism was notable for its two kinds of meetings: the four-day meetings and the camp meetings. Four-day meetings were gatherings of clergy and lay members for prayer, preaching and lecturing, while the church leaders discussed church business. The four-day meetings were usually held in cities.

Camp meetings were different. They could last up to a week and were held outdoors, far away from cities and towns, with the hundreds of attendees staying in tents. Much like the four-day meetings, there was the usual preaching and praying and lecturing, but camp meetings were marked by an intensity unseen in meetings held in cities. The woods around the campgrounds echoed with the shouted pleas for salvation.

Critics saw camp meetings as breeding grounds for fanaticism. Author Catherine Williams, who would later take up Sarah's cause, visited a camp meeting in Rhode Island and reported that "all was hubbub and confusion." Poorly spoken preachers addressed the crowds, hysterical women fell to the ground in convulsions, men consorted with "women of most infamous character" and fights broke out. Williams was told to come back for evening prayers, as the meetings were that much more "powerful" after dark. Many rose early and stayed up late into the night, spending the entire meeting in a state of near exhaustion. Each camp meeting also famously attracted a rogues' gallery of pickpockets, drunks, con artists and gawking townies.

Of course, not every camp meeting could be quite as over-the-top as what Williams described, which occasionally borders on Maria Monk territory. I suspect for most attendees, a camp meeting passed without incident and was a positive, uplifting experience of faith with other members of the faithful.

Like other ministers of the church, Avery had accepted a series of assignments at various congregations around the region, some lasting up to two years. This system of rotating personnel somewhat resembled Methodism's early days, when the word was spread by itinerant preachers and "circuit riders," who rode through town every few months to minister to the flock. By the time he was assigned to Lowell in June 1830, Avery had advanced through the clerical hierarchy to attain the rank of elder.

Avery arrived in Bristol, Rhode Island, with his wife and young family on July 4, 1832. He had been sent to resuscitate the town's languishing Methodist congregation. Bristol is a pleasant seaport town, at that time about the same size as Tiverton, where the old money families largely owed their wealth to the slave trade. It also boasts the nation's oldest Independence Day parade, but there was no parade that year, so things may have been relatively quiet as the steamship dropped him off at the dock. He must have limped along the dock, as he had hurt his ankle—dislocating it or possibly even breaking it—while jumping over a fence, just before leaving Lowell.

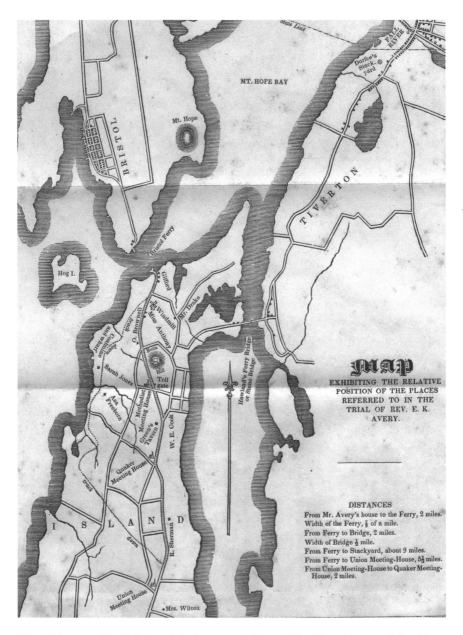

Map of the scene. Durfee's farm is in the upper right and Bristol is to the upper left, with the northern end of Aquidneck Island in the middle. *Courtesy Brown University.*

Bidwell knew his way around Bristol as he looked for Avery, as he himself had been stationed there some time before. It's unclear how long the two men had been acquainted, but they seemed to know each other well. They spent time together now that they were in proximity, even recently trading ministerial duties, with Avery taking to Bidwell's pulpit in Fall River while Bidwell preached to Avery's congregation in Bristol.

Probably finding Avery at the meetinghouse, away from his wife and children, Bidwell brought him into a quiet room to inform him that Sarah Cornell was dead. He quickly described the events of that morning, perhaps laying particular emphasis on Dr. Wilbur's statement that Sarah claimed to be pregnant with Avery's child as a result of an illicit affair.

Avery was shocked, insisting that this was "altogether untrue," adding that he was "prepared to meet anything of the kind."

Bidwell spent the night at Avery's house, and the two of them must have been up late into the night discussing matters and possible courses of action. They planned to go together to Lowell on Monday to make inquiries about Sarah's "bad character" that might help dispel any suspicions about Avery's supposed involvement with the young woman.

Bidwell left the next morning, returning to the stack yard to denounce Sarah and refuse to take responsibility for burying her. Avery wrote to another Methodist minister, Samuel Drake of Portsmouth, asking him to come to Bristol at once. Drake arrived about noon, and Avery outlined the situation, admitting that he had been away from home on the evening of December 20, the night when Sarah must have hanged herself. He had taken a long walk on Aquidneck Island—he was known for his long rambles—and had been forced to spend the night on the island when the ferryman refused to carry him back to Bristol so late at night.

This by itself was not all that damning or even suggestive. However, once arriving on Aquidneck Island from Bristol, it was a short walk across the northern tip of the island to a bridge that connected Aquidneck to Tiverton. On the night in question, Avery was only a bridge away from where Sarah Cornell died.

CHAPTER 4

"From Strong Circumstantial Evidence"

Meanwhile, back in Tiverton, a significant discovery was made just a few hours after Sarah's burial.

One of the women who had examined the body was sorting through the things in Sarah's bandbox when she found a note written in pencil on a small folded slip of paper:

> *If I should be missing enquire of the Rev. Mr. Avery of Bristol he will know where I am. Dec. 20th. S.M. Cornell.*

She brought the note to Durfee late Saturday afternoon. He had noticed it when looking through Sarah's belongings but passed it by unread. It was only a little scrap of folded-up paper and probably didn't seem important at the time. But it was.

Durfee brought it to Hicks on Sunday morning, and the coroner summoned the jury once again.

The discovery of the note, dated the day of her death, began to suggest a very different version of events. Clearly, Avery was more closely involved than had been previously supposed. Perhaps Sarah had not been in that field alone on Friday night. Perhaps she had been keeping an appointment or even an assignation.

Two men of the jury had to be replaced when it was found that they were not "freeholders"—landowners—and under Rhode Island law could not sit on a jury. Because of this, there was some question if the verdict the jury had returned earlier was even legal.

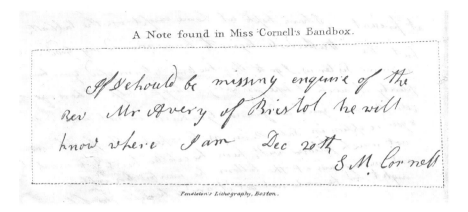

A Note found in Miss Cornell's Bandbox.

If I should be missing enquire of the Rev Mr Avery of Bristol he will know where I am Dec 20th
S M Cornell

Pendleton's Lithography, Boston.

Facsimile of the pencil note found in Sarah's bandbox that first raised suspicions of foul play. *Courtesy Brown University.*

Perhaps deciding that a more thorough investigation was called for, Hicks ordered the body of Sarah Cornell to be exhumed and autopsied first thing Monday morning. He told the jury to be on hand to consider the results of the autopsy and the new evidence of the pencil note.

Hicks issued his instructions on Sunday morning, but rather than wait until the next day, John Durfee took matters into his own hands. After conversing with Dr. Wilbur on the day before, Durfee had been among those who suspected foul play. Probably assuming that a new verdict of murder was inevitable, he set off for Bristol in search of a warrant for the minister's arrest.

Upon reaching Bristol, he applied to Justice Samuel Coggeshall, but the elderly Coggeshall was not a justice of the peace and could not issue an arrest warrant. Durfee then approached Justice John Howe. Howe considered their application and issued the warrant.

Normally, a coroner needed to have the verdict of his jury stating that they had determined a crime had been committed before a justice would issue an arrest warrant. Why Durfee, a private citizen, could manage to wrangle such a warrant out of a justice is anybody's guess. As he stood in Howe's office that Sunday morning, there was not even legal recognition that a murder had been committed, let alone that Avery was a suspect.

Still, a warrant for Reverend Avery's arrest on suspicion of murder was delivered to Bristol County deputy sheriff William Paul.

On Sunday, December 23, Avery was arrested at home about sunset. Word had already reached him earlier that day, when the stagecoach arrived from Fall River bearing the news that he was now a suspect—gossip having

The Bristol town jail, where Avery spent one night, is today the headquarters of the Bristol Historical and Preservation Society. The building was constructed of ship ballast stones in 1823. *Photo by Robert O'Brien.*

apparently hardened into fact for some. When the warrant was read out to him, Avery blanched, his knees buckled as he steadied himself against the furniture and he simply said, "I submit to the laws."

He lawyered up and spent the night in the town's stone jail, praying.

Monday morning was a busy one.

In Bristol, Avery was escorted from his cell to the courthouse just up the street. It was only a short walk, but on that morning it must have seemed endless to him. He was arraigned and a preliminary hearing was scheduled. This hearing was to determine which court had jurisdiction and if there was probable cause to charge him with murder. The hearing would commence the next day, Tuesday, December 25. In early, still-Puritanical New England, Christmas Day was not a civic holiday. Handling the case would be Justice John Howe, the same man who had issued the warrant for Avery's arrest, and Justice Levi Haile.

The court allowed Avery a small mercy and sent him home to his family. He would not have to spend another night in the town jail, but one of Paul's men would be keeping a watchful eye on him.

In Tiverton, Sarah's body was exhumed and brought to Durfee's barn. Dr. Wilbur and another doctor named Foster Hooper began an autopsy while the jury looked on. Wilbur felt that the first examination, conducted by several local matrons with no medical training, could hardly be called an examination at all. The two physicians proceeded cautiously.

The cord had left a deep red mark around her neck where it had bitten into the flesh. Wilbur and Hooper determined that the cause of death was strangulation and not a broken neck, which was usually the cause in suicides by hanging. They noted the hand-shaped bruises around the hips that the women had mentioned before, along with the scratches and grass stains on the knees. The jury balked when the doctors moved to strip the body completely, apparently wishing to allow Sarah at least some dignity, even in death.

Opening the abdomen and the uterus, they found a fetus approximately four and a half months old. Sarah Cornell had been pregnant with a daughter.

The physicians reported their findings to the jury as the body was reinterred. After some deliberation, the six men reached a verdict that everyone at this point was expecting anyway:

> *And said jurors upon their oaths as aforesaid further say, that the said Sarah M. Cornell came by her death by having a cord or a hemp line drawn around her neck and strangled until she was dead and then hung on a stake in a stack yard belonging to Richard Durfee, in Tiverton, State of Rhode Island, they also believe, and from strong circumstantial evidence, that Ephraim K. Avery, of Bristol, in the County of Bristol, and State of &c. was principal or accessory in her death. And so the jurors aforesaid, &c. do say that the said Ephraim K. Avery in manner and form aforesaid, of his malice aforethought, the said Sarah M. Cornell did kill and murder or cause to be killed and murdered, against the peace, RICHARD DURFEE, (et al).*

In Fall River, a boy ran through the streets, ringing a bell. News of the suspected murder had been discussed in taverns, churches and parlors, in the mills and at the dinner tables throughout the city all weekend. Now a meeting was being called to discuss the situation. No one knows who sent the boy or who called the meeting, but the Lyceum Hall was soon packed with an anxious public. Some two hundred citizens crowded into the building that night.

After hours of considering and loudly debating their options, the citizenry of Fall River voted to assist the Rhode Island authorities in their investigations. In 1832, Rhode Island had no organized police force (neither did Fall River; in fact, they wouldn't even have a night watch for another decade). Law and order was enforced by county sheriffs who gathered posses as needed and were always open to outside help.

She may have only lived there a short time, but Sarah Cornell was one of Fall River's own, and something needed to be done.

They organized two committees and elected officers. The first was the Committee of Investigation, consisting of five men "to aid and assist the authorities of Rhode Island in having the subject properly investigated, and in prosecuting it to a final issue." One of the men elected to serve on the committee was Dr. Hooper, probably just returned from performing the autopsy and reporting his findings to those gathered at the Lyceum. Another was Nathaniel Briggs Borden, a Fall River businessman, politician and relative of Lizzie Borden.

Also chosen for the Committee of Investigation was a deputy sheriff, Colonel Harvey Harnden. Approaching forty years of age, Harnden brought with him years of experience and a certain amount of legal authority to

Fall River, circa 1840. To the right is the new Methodist church, built after Sarah's death. While she never saw that building, the rest of the street is probably much as she knew it during her short time in town. *Courtesy Fall River Historical Society.*

what might otherwise be seen as a rabble of self-appointed amateur sleuths. We know very little about him or his background, which is probably what he would have preferred, but his actions in the investigation would show him to be a tenacious, hard-nosed detective.

Working under, and answerable to, the five men in the first group was the larger and more ominously named Committee of Vigilance. We don't know how many official members this group had, as the membership list is long lost; it may have been a dozen, and it may have been many more. They swore to assist in the "ferreting out of who committed the offense" and were instructed to hand over to the first committee "any evidence or circumstances that might have come to their knowledge, having a bearing upon the case." They maintained that they were searching for the truth.

But really, their minds were already made up, and they were looking for evidence to convict Avery.

Sarah had lived in Fall River for a scant two months. She was one of countless more or less anonymous mill girls working in the factories and far from a pillar of the community, so it is unclear why the citizens of Fall River reacted to her death with such organized outrage. One explanation that has been offered is that her murder gave the mill owners a black eye, suggesting that women coming to work in their mills were not safe. The mill owners could not allow such bad publicity, as it would stem the flow of young women coming to them looking for work, so they moved to swiftly bring the guilty to justice.

While this is an intriguing explanation, I have been unable to find anyone at the time articulating this point of view, so as with so many other aspects of this story, motives remain uncertain.

CHAPTER 5

"Don't Ruin Me Here"

The minister appeared in court on Christmas morning to give his statement. The justices hearing the case warned him that he was not required to make a statement and that if it were later contradicted by facts, it could prove damaging.

Upon his arrest, Avery had requested Bristol's Nathaniel Bullock take his case, but Bullock's heavy workload prevented him from being present that morning, and he advised that Avery retrain his colleague Mr. Blake to handle the preliminaries. Blake now stood with him before the bench, with the minister's written statement in hand. They had been up half the night, going over it again and again.

Avery first crossed paths with Sarah Cornell in July 1830, one month after his arrival in Lowell. She was then going by Maria, as she often did. He had noticed her in the congregation—the pretty, vivacious Sarah probably stood out in any crowd—but had had no particular contact with her until she came to his home one day, looking for work as a domestic. She may have been hoping for a break from the noisy, often strenuous life of the mills.

"Mrs. Avery not being pleased with her appearance, she was not engaged," he said. However, others later stated that she had in fact worked for the family for a few weeks before being let go.

In August, Sarah requested a certificate of regular standing in the church, as she planned to attend a Methodist meeting on Cape Cod before traveling to Killingly, Connecticut, to visit friends.

Bristol County Courthouse, where Avery's hearing was held. The building dates to 1816 and was designed by Russell Warren, who also designed the Arcade in downtown Providence. *Photo by Robert O'Brien.*

Since his arrival in town, Avery had heard some troubling things about Sarah. There were rumors that she was a thief, and she apparently had a tendency toward colorful profanity—perhaps something she had picked up in the mills. He hesitated to grant her request for a certificate but agreed to issue one on the condition that she watch her mouth at the meeting on the Cape. If he did not receive a good report of her conduct, he would write to the minister in Killingly, instructing him to refuse Sarah's admittance to his church during her stay there. Apparently, she spent her time on the Cape quietly and then proceeded to Connecticut without incident.

Back in Lowell, Sarah obtained a job in one of the many mills, and Avery was soon approached by a factory overseer who passed along a report from one of his clerks saying that Sarah was a bad character. Allegedly, she had even stated to him directly that Sarah had been "guilty of illicit intercourse with two or more."

Within a day or two, Sarah once again appeared on Avery's doorstep. The overseer had warned her that if she did not go tell Avery, he would himself.

She had hesitated, and the man acted. Now she was here to confess her sins to her minister. She was indeed guilty of sleeping with a young man.

Avery, perhaps meeting her confession with a stern face and an arched eyebrow, told her he had heard it was at least two men. Sarah broke down and admitted that was correct. She asked what course of action would be taken now.

He said that as an unmarried woman she of course must be tried before the church on charges of fornication. He advised that it might be best for her to be tried in absentia and that she had best leave town and stay with friends if possible until the trial was over.

It is probably safe to suppose that the two young men were not reported to their ministers, nor were charged in their churches.

Before she left, Avery demanded the return of the certificate he had issued previously. Sarah replied, shamefacedly, that she had lost it on the Cape. She left for Dover, New Hampshire, later that same day.

After her departure, a local physician, Dr. Graves, also came calling on Avery, stating that Sarah had consulted him for treatment of "the foul disease"—gonorrhea—and that "her case was as aggravated as any he had ever known—that she could not sit or stand still, and walked with difficulty." Graves felt it was his duty to inform the minister. Avery then compounded the doctor's questionable behavior by repeating this information to the tribunal convened to try Sarah on charges of fornication.

With Sarah gone and not on hand to defend herself or even be heard, she was unsurprisingly found guilty and expelled from the Lowell church. For perhaps obvious reasons, Sarah apparently decided that Dover suited her better than Lowell and applied for membership in the Methodist congregation there. When making her application to Reverend Dow, she submitted her certificate of regular standing from the Lowell church—the same certificate she'd told Avery had been lost on the Cape.

Hearing of this, an outraged Avery fired off two letters. The first was to Reverend Dow, warning him of Sarah's character. The second went to Sarah herself, demanding the return of the certificate and threatening her with public exposure should she fail to comply.

She mailed back the certificate.

Reverend Dow wrote, asking for details, which Avery supplied.

Ruined in Dover, Sarah moved to Great Falls, New Hampshire, attending services in Reverend Storrs's church. Perhaps wishing to make a clean break, she eventually wrote to Avery. Much of what was said about her was true, she said. She had been a "bad girl" and had slept with several men. She insisted that she had never been afflicted with "the foul disease" and in turn accused Graves of making improper advances while he examined her.

Avery ignored the letter.

A few days later, having attended a sermon in which Reverend Storrs exhorted his parishioners to confess their sins, she again wrote to her former minister "to make a fuller acknowledgement of her crimes—that she had been guilty of all the crimes charged upon her," adding that she had unknowingly contracted "the foul disease."

This letter also went unanswered.

On a Sunday morning in the spring of 1831, Sarah appeared at Avery's door. She had written seeking his forgiveness, she said, and when he had not replied she made the trip to Lowell to see him in person. Avery must have ushered her into his study embarrassedly, casting a quick glance out into the street before slamming the door behind him.

"Forgiveness from me means nothing," he admonished. "You must seek it from the Lord."

She asked for his forgiveness in writing. She seemed so pathetic, tearful and begging that he felt her attempts to reform her previously bad character must be sincere. He wrote her a letter offering his forgiveness. The gift of repentance, he reasoned, must not be denied.

Sarah left with his letter in hand, and he probably thought she was finally out of his life at last. He was wrong.

In August 1832, he attended a camp meeting at Thompson, Connecticut. One night in the ministers' tent, Presiding Elder Abraham Merrill mentioned that there were "bad characters" on the campground. Perhaps Merrill was referring to one of the unwelcome troublemakers who seemed to appear at every camp meeting. It soon became clear, however, that he meant Sarah Cornell, among others.

Avery noticed her shortly after Merrill made his comment, but he did not speak to her.

Two months later found Avery visiting Reverend Bidwell in Fall River as the leaves turned red and gold against the graying October sky. He was in the mill town for another four-day meeting. Bidwell inquired if he knew a Sarah Cornell, and Avery replied, probably guardedly, that he had known a Maria Cornell in Lowell. Further discussion revealed that they were talking about the same woman, now a member of Bidwell's congregation. Bidwell expected as much.

One night during his stay in Fall River, Avery felt a tug at his sleeve and turned to find Sarah at his elbow.

"What do you want?" he asked.

"To speak with you."

"But I have nothing to say to you."

"But I *must* speak with you."

Excusing himself from his companions for a moment, he moved her a few steps away and asked what she wanted.

"I have come to live here in Fall River where I am not known and don't want you to expose me."

"I have no disposition to injure you," Avery replied. "And it will depend entirely on your own behavior if I expose you or not."

"Don't ruin me here," Sarah insisted. "You ruined me in Lowell, you ruined me in Dover—but don't here."

"I have certainly not ruined you—you have ruined yourself."

"I have joined a class here on trial, and if you do not tell brother Bidwell about what happened before he will never know."

Avery waved dismissively, once again saying that her future depended upon her own behavior. With that, he left her, shaking his head as he went.

He noticed her in the congregation a few weeks later, when Bidwell once again brought him to Fall River as a guest preacher. They did not speak, and according to him that was the last time he saw her.

Events would show that Avery's account of his history with Sarah Cornell was, by and large, accurate.

But he also left out certain significant details.

CHAPTER 6

"ATTENDED BY THE MOST AGGRAVATED CIRCUMSTANCES"

Court adjourned and Avery went home for the day. Later that afternoon, the Fall River Committee of Vigilance arrived in Bristol like the marines hitting Omaha Beach. They crossed Mount Hope Bay aboard the *King Philip*, coincidentally the same steamboat that had brought Avery to Bristol back in July.

Elihu Hicks led the charge, brandishing the new verdict accusing Avery of murder. He slammed it down on the desk of Justice Howe, demanding that the minister be handed over at once. He asserted that as Tiverton, the scene of the crime, was in Newport County, the authorities of Bristol, in Bristol County, could not claim Avery as their prisoner. He ignored the fact that John Durfee, a private citizen, had obtained an arrest warrant from this same judge without the authority to do so, as this only confused matters further. Howe looked down his nose at Hicks, weighed his options and said he would look into it. To his credit, he actually did, even writing to Rhode Island attorney general Albert C. Greene for advice. But ultimately, his answer would be no—Bristol had him, and they wouldn't let go. The case would be heard in Bristol.

Harvey Harnden visited Nathaniel Bullock's office and demanded an interview with the accused. He didn't have any more luck than Hicks was having elsewhere, but the argument was cut short when the door banged open and a panicked, breathless man entered the lawyer's office.

There was an angry mob, "a multitude," making its way through the streets of Bristol, headed for Avery's house. The minister's life was in danger, the man yelled, and he had been sent by the watchful Deputy Paul to summon the lawyer. He must come at once.

Bullock and Harnden left together and arrived at Avery's house within a few minutes. A large crowd, consisting of the Committee of Vigilance and probably numerous hangers-on and the idly curious, surrounded the building where Avery lived. This came as no surprise to Harnden, as he had come over with them all on the *King Philip*, but it must have shocked Bullock. Onlookers later estimated the crowd at 100 or 150. According to one witness, they resembled "men out of the factories, and some, by their dress, I took were the selectmen of Fall River." The supposed selectmen were identified by their long coats and tight pantaloons, the attire of a well-dressed dandy.

Although large and noisy, the crowd was not directly violent. But they did make their demands.

"Give us Avery!" someone shouted. "We'll have him dead or alive!"

"I'll shoot him through the window!" cried another. It was an idle threat, as he didn't have a gun.

"The courthouse can't hold him—Bristol can't hold him—the trial should be in Tiverton where he killed the girl!"

"We'll hang him!"

A knot of men pushed through the back door and into the sink room of the house, demanding to see Avery. A few others escorted John Orswell, the engineer from the *King Philip*, into the house. Avery, who had been hiding upstairs, came down to face the engineer, and a brief, tense interview took place before Orswell left, nodding his head. Few at the time knew exactly what had transpired, but the meeting in the sink room that day would later prove to be an important episode.

According to Bullock's account, he remained at the edge of the crowd, observing, for the duration of the thirty-minute standoff. But according to Harnden, Bullock had hung back, saying that he thought he had gone far enough, and watched nervously for a few minutes before retreating back to the safety of his office.

The *King Philip*'s bell rang, signaling its imminent departure, and the crowd headed back to the dock, leaving the streets once again quiet and the citizens of Bristol badly shaken.

The story hit the newspapers that same day.

The 1830s were a rough-and-tumble time in the history of journalism. Editors attacked one another in print and even occasionally in the street.

Competition was fierce, and often stories were lifted verbatim from other newspapers without credit or compunction; indeed, it was once said that the editor's most valuable tools were a pair of scissors and a jar of paste. Papers were partisan and polemic and of course never let the facts stand in the way of a good story.

Most newspapers consisted of a single folded sheet, making four pages. The front page was usually given over to advertisements or occasionally political or even religious screeds reprinted from other sources. Actual news was on page two, and page three often featured a mix of ads, poetry, humor, fiction and short man-bites-dog news items. Sometimes this spilled over onto the back page, with the rest of the space being taken up once again with advertisements. There were no illustrations aside from a very few in the advertisements—just columns and columns of tiny, close-packed print.

On December 25, 1832, the *Providence Journal*, exorbitantly priced at six and a quarter cents per issue, broke the story:

> OUTRAGE AND MURDER—*We learn, very direct, that a murder, attended by the most aggravated circumstances, has been recently committed, in the edge of the town of Tiverton, near Fall River. A young woman, residing in Bristol, was some time since seduced by a minister of the Methodist denomination stationed at Bristol, named AVERILL, whose ministrations she attended. We learn that he first fabricated irreligious charges against her, and effected his wicked purpose, by defending her and helping her out of the difficulties which he induced her to believe existed. She became* enceinte [pregnant], *and went to Fall River to reside. Here she wrote to her betrayer, who returned her an answer, advising her to go to an apothecary, and enquire for a drug—the oil of tansy—and to take it—being careful "not to consult a doctor." She however proceeded to a physician—enjoined upon him the strictest secrecy—and then informed him of her situation, and the advice which she had received—He told her, that the drug would cause her instant death. She then addressed Averill a letter saying that she could not follow his directions. He returned an answer requesting her to meet him at nightfall near Bristol. She showed this letter to the physician, who advised her not to grant the interview. She therefore did not. She soon however received another letter, stating his intention to convey her out of town, where she could enjoy a privacy in confinement, necessary to preserve her reputation—and urging her to meet him in the edge of Tiverton, with a cloak and calash, that she might not be recognized. She went, as requested. The next morning, her lifeless body—bearing marks of violence, and resisted force—was found*

suspended by a rope, thrown over the top of a pole of a hay stack. Her comb, and locks of her hair were found at a considerable distance from the stack,—and her situation was such, that no doubt could exist, but she had been willfully murdered. The minister, it is said, crossed Bristol ferry, late in the evening, and then returned on the next morning—Saturday—on which forenoon the body was discovered. Averill has been committed to Bristol jail. We may hope, that the report is somewhat exaggerated—although it reaches us in no "questionable shape."

Like the Committee of Vigilance, the *Providence Journal* had clearly already made up its editorial mind. The report certainly was exaggerated, a mixture of fact and fiction, containing a few nuggets of good information scattered among rumor and guesswork. The reporter didn't know on which day Sarah's body had been discovered and didn't even get Avery's name right. In cobbling together a half-true version of events and passing it along to the public, the anonymous reporter undoubtedly swayed public opinion against Avery; the public must have reasoned (as many still do today) that if it was in the newspaper it must be true.

CHAPTER 7

"Such a Distinct and Perfect Chain of Testimony"

The hearing proper began the next day. John Durfee was the first witness called, and he related his discovery of the body, his conversation with the landlady and the finding of the letters. Dr. Wilbur testified to Sarah's consulting him in the weeks leading up to her death. When prosecutor William Staples asked why Sarah had consulted him, the court interjected, saying the doctor was not allowed to answer. Justices Howe and Haile did not elaborate on their prohibition. Staples had hit his first snag—Wilbur could not mention Sarah's pregnancy nor her disclosure that Avery was the father.

Thomas Hart and Benjamin Manchester testified to finding pieces of a broken comb some distance from the body, amid rose bushes and "pudding stones." The comb was later identified by Lucy Hathaway as belonging to Sarah, who was wearing it when she left the mill on December 20. The comb was probably a prized possession, perhaps a gift, as Sarah had once taken the trouble to fix it when it had broken—witnesses commented on the repair work done with two small rivets. That the pieces of the comb were found in an area with wild rose bushes suggests that perhaps this had been the scene of a struggle and that the rose thorns were the cause of the scratches on her knees.

Elihu Hicks was called and gave a brief outline of his jury's actions and decision. He then produced the letters found among Sarah's effects.

Staples knew he had to show that Avery was more intimately connected to Sarah Cornell than his statement suggested. Over the next few days, he called

The courtroom where Avery's probable cause hearing was held. *Photo by Robert O'Brien.*

several witnesses to piece together the story of the clandestine relationship between the minister and the mill girl.

Seth Darling, the elderly postmaster of Fall River, was called to the stand. In addition to being a member of the Committee of Vigilance, he had been among the curious crowd gathered at Durfee's farm that awful morning. He had, in fact, accompanied John Durfee to Sarah's boardinghouse later that day and also had been at Durfee's side when he applied to Justice Howe for the arrest warrant.

According to Darling's testimony, on November 19 he had been making up the day's mail and had just removed several letters from the mailbox there in the post office and was sorting them by destination when he heard something drop into the box behind him. Turning, he found two letters, one addressed to Grindall Rawson in Connecticut and the other addressed to Bristol. The seal on the letter to Bristol was still wet. Searching his memory, Darling thought it might have been addressed to Reverend Avery, but he couldn't quite be sure. Unfortunately, he did not see who deposited the letters when his back was turned.

By itself, this proved nothing other than that someone in Fall River wrote to someone in Bristol and Connecticut. Given that one of the letters was addressed to Grindall Rawson, it is easy to suppose—and many indeed did suppose—that Sarah wrote both letters and that the Bristol letter was intended for Reverend Avery.

Lucy Hathaway, daughter of Sarah's landlady, worked with Sarah at the Fall River Manufactory, also as a weaver operating a water-powered loom. She testified that "a week or a fortnight from the Sabbath before her death, in the morning, she asked me this question—Lucy, do you think it's possible for an innocent young girl to be led away by a man that she has confidence in, and rather looks up to?"

Lucy hesitated and said, "I don't know."

"But what can an innocent girl do in the hands of a strong man?" Sarah asked. "And he using all kinds of argument?"

Now Lucy didn't know what to say. When the subject of camp meetings was raised later in their conversation, Sarah said that she had been to many but would never go again.

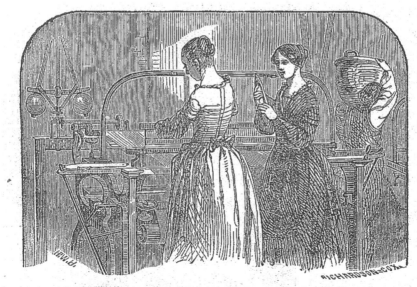

POWER LOOM. ONE GIRL ATTENDS FOUR.

Two mill girls at work on their looms. *Courtesy Larry DePetrillo.*

"Why, Sarah?" Lucy asked.

"Because I have seen things transacted there that would condemn them to my mind."

When pressed for further explanation, Sarah would only say that something had happened between a married minister and a church member.

She further complained that she had not felt well since the Thompson camp meeting in August.

John Orswell, engineer onboard the *King Philip*, also had a story to tell. His boat ran between Fall River and Providence, carrying goods and passengers. It left Fall River for Providence at ten o'clock on Mondays, Wednesday and Fridays, making the trip from Providence to Fall River on Tuesdays, Thursdays and Saturdays. The boat stopped at Bristol each way. Tickets cost fifty cents, and newspaper advertisements described the boat as "splendid."

In the last week of November, when preparing to leave Providence, Orswell was tending to his usual duties and probably trying to keep warm. Winter was coming—the air was cold and the water was cold. It would be warmer back in the engine room, with the boiler. He was headed aft when he saw a man on the dock, trying to get his attention.

The man was dressed in a sober dark cloak and hat. He seemed very intent on speaking with the engineer, and Orswell approached.

The man held up a letter on pink paper and asked Orswell to take it to Fall River and hand deliver it for him. Orswell refused—crew members were prohibited from carrying letters. He pointed to the mailbox on deck. The man could deposit his letter there, and the post office would take care of it.

But the man in the cloak was adamant—Orswell *must* take the letter for him. The engineer again refused, and the man, probably with a nervous glance around him, took a coin from his pocket and handed it over with the letter. It was ninepence.

Welcome, for a moment, to the bewildering world of coinage in the early republic. National standardized paper money was just a distant dream, and most paper money was printed, issued and backed by local banks. Although the banks printed dollars, many Americans still thought in terms of pounds, shillings and pence; occasionally, price lists (especially in New England) gave prices in both dollars and pounds. Coins were a different matter, and a wide variety of foreign coins were used in everyday transactions. To add to the confusion, the ninepence Orswell refers to is probably not even an English

Providence Nov 1831

No 5

Dear Sister

I received your letter in due season and should have answered it before now but thought I would wait till this of Trinity — as I told you I am willing to help you and do for yo as circumstances are I should rather you you would come to the place viz Bristol in the stage the 18th if December and stop at the Hotell and stay till 6 in in the evening and then go up directly across the main street to a brick building nevre to the stone meeting house where I will meet you and talk with you when you stop at the tavern either inquire for work or go on to the street in pretense of looking for some or something else and I may see you say nothing about meer my fami should it storm on the 18 come the 20th — if you cannot come and it will be more convenient to meet me at the methodist meeting house in summerset just over the ferry on either of the above eve'g I will meet you there at the same hour or if you cannot do either I will come to fall river on one of the above evenings back of the same meeting house where I once saw you at any house you say on either of the above evenings when there will be the least passing I should think before the mills stop work this I will leave with you if I come I will come if it does not storm very hard if it does the first ill come the second write me soon and tell me which — when you write direct your letter to Betsey Hills Bristol and not as you have to me remember this your last letter I am afraid was broken open were your eelash not your plain bonni you can send your letter by mail Yours &c B. He

Sister C

Facsimile of the pink letter Orswell received from the stranger. *Courtesy Brown University.*

coin, but likely a Spanish real from one of the South American colonies that Americans valued at twelve and a half cents.

Orswell pocketed the coin and the letter. Working as an engineer on a steamboat was backbreaking work—he was probably always too hot or too cold and always dirty from the coal-fired boiler. On the water all day, he could never quite get dry. He probably felt he deserved a little bit more than he usually got, and what harm could there be in dropping off a letter for someone? As the man retreated quickly down the dock, Orswell slid the letter into his jacket and made his way to the engine room to get to work. It was almost time to depart.

Arriving in Fall River, he stepped off the gangplank and checked the address. It read simply "Miss Sarah M. Connell, Fall River, Mass. To be left at Mrs. Cole's." He'd accidentally smeared some oil "smut" from his fingers on it. Ascertaining where Mrs. Cole's was, he set off through streets of the busy mill town.

Mrs. Cole's turned out to be a modest boardinghouse. She was out, so he left the letter with her husband, Elijah. It was nearly sundown, and Sarah had not yet returned from the mill. Mr. Cole left the letter in the window, where it would no doubt be noticed, and told his daughter about it. According to Elijah Cole, Sarah picked the letter up the next day.

Later, Orswell could not quite recall exactly when this took place. It was, he said, either the twenty-eighth or twenty-ninth of November. As the boat was docked in Providence and about to leave for Fall River, it must have been Thursday the twenty-ninth.

Submitting the pink letter to the justices, Staples remarked that it was dated "Providence, Nov. 1831." Obviously, he observed, it should have been dated 1832. This is the letter outlining plans for a secret meeting, with assurances that "I am willing to help you and do for you." It also cautions, "When you write direct your letters to Mrs. Betsey Hills, Bristol, and not as you have to me. Remember this. Your last letter I am afraid was broken open."

The letter closed with a cryptic remark, scrawled on the outside: "Let me enjoin the secret. Keep the letters in your bosom or burn them up."

The defense, of course, denied that Avery had anything to do with the letter. But who was the man who insisted the engineer hand deliver this unusual missive?

Orswell had heard the rumors that a Methodist minister was suspected in Sarah's death. He remembered that the day the man in the cloak appeared on the dock, the Methodists in Providence were hosting a four-day meeting, attracting members and ministers from miles around, as these meetings always did. He must have mentioned this, possibly when the Committee of Vigilance was on the *King Philip* bound for Bristol, and he was asked if he could identify the man he had seen. On Christmas Day, he was brought to Avery's house and was among those who pushed their way into the sink room.

Face to face with the minister, Orswell recognized him as the same man who had pressed the pink letter and ninepence into his hand.

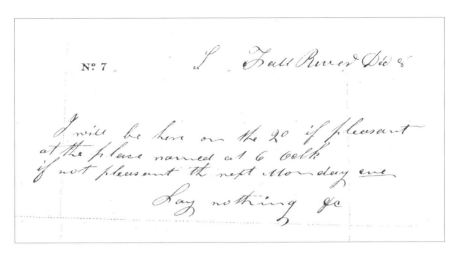

Facsimile of the letter written on half a sheet of white paper from Iram Smith's store, setting an assignation. *Courtesy Brown University.*

The white letter, dated Fall River, December 8, was written on a half-sheet of white paper and clearly confirmed an assignation. It read, "I will be here on the 20th if pleasant at the place named at 6 o'clock if not pleasant the next Monday eve.—say nothing."

Iram Smith was the proprietor of a recently opened variety store on Pleasant Street in Fall River, near the stagecoach office. He advertised "A general assortment of family groceries, dry goods, essences, etc., also Gordack's pills and drops." He also sold paper.

On December 8, Avery was in Fall River visiting with his colleague, Reverend Bidwell. According to Iram Smith and a customer shopping in the store at the time, the two ministers were in the store that day. Smith, no doubt busy with the dozens of things a Yankee shopkeeper did on the average day, did not have a very clear recollection of events but did his best to describe what he remembered.

Avery and Bidwell had been discussing an article in the newspaper, the *Fall River Weekly Recorder*. Avery seemed to take exception to something in the article and asserted that he would write a letter to the editor voicing his opinion. Smith did not know what article had so provoked the minister.

Avery asked for a piece of paper for his letter. Apparently, Smith was too busy and Avery helped himself to half a sheet and brought it over to Smith's desk to write. Neither Smith nor Jeremy Howland, the customer who also testified, could swear that Avery wrote anything while in the store, but both thought he could have.

Avery asked for a wafer—an adhesive paper disc to seal the letter. Smith was out of wafers and quickly ran next door to get one. Bidwell left the store just ahead of Avery, who caught the stagecoach for the nearby town of New Bedford on an errand, returning to Fall River to preach that evening at Bidwell's church.

Once the hearing was underway in Bristol, Harvey Harnden went to Smith's variety store and demanded to see all the paper he had for sale. Sifting through the paper in stock, they found half a sheet shoved about halfway down in a ream of paper. Harnden took possession of the half-sheet after clearly marking it in Smith's presence for future identification. He later compared it with the December 8 letter to Sarah Cornell, going so far as to examine them "through a microscope," and the two pieces matched, ragged edge, watermarks and all.

The defense objected. It had not been proven that Avery wrote the letters. Smith and Howland weren't certain that Avery had written anything—they thought he might have, but they hadn't positively seen him doing do. Showing matching edges and watermarks was one thing, but it was not evidence of who wrote the letters in the first place, which was surely the more important question. The court agreed, adding that they had no opposition to the letter being read aloud, but no inferences as to authorship would be drawn. If there was proof of the authorship of the letters, let it be brought forth.

To that end, Bidwell was put on the stand, but he maintained that he was "not very fully acquainted" with Avery's handwriting. He dismissed the pink letter as looking like a woman's writing and admitted that he had recently received a letter from Avery on paper similar to the yellow letter that had been found in Sarah's bandbox along with the others.

Isaac Fiske, a local "teacher of writing" with "more or less a dozen years" of experience, was called to examine the letters and study the handwriting. He pointed out the differences and the similarities in the three letters and in the end judged that "the letters were all written by the same person, in a feigned hand." One of them—though it is not clear from court transcripts which letter he is referring to—had the "design of imitating a female hand."

Grindall Rawson, Sarah's brother-in-law, came from his home in Woodstock, Connecticut, to testify. Sarah had come to stay with him and his wife, her sister, in June and remained through October. A few weeks after arriving for her visit, Sarah went to work in Rawson's tailoring shop, doing her usual seamstress work and also, later, the bookkeeping. There were no Methodists nearby, so Sarah may have felt somewhat isolated and was no doubt happy to hear that a camp meeting was to be held in the town of Thompson, only a few miles away. She arranged for a few days off—which is probably easier when the boss is married to your sister—and arrived at the camp meeting in the last week of August.

Avery was there, as he himself had admitted in his opening statement.

Finally, Staples had reached a key moment in the story he was constructing. If the court would not allow Wilbur's testimony to be heard, much the same information could be gotten from Grindall Rawson. Almost casually, Staples asked, "Did you hear Maria, before she left your house for the last time in October last, say what her condition was?"

Bullock must have been on his feet to object before Rawson could even open his mouth to answer the question. Bullock insisted that no declarations of the deceased, especially any of her accusations against the defendant, should be admitted, unless they came under the heading of "dying declarations," which none of Sarah's did. The court agreed. Staples must have been furious—the court refused to admit Wilbur's testimony about Sarah's "condition," they had practically ignored the letters and now Rawson was prevented from giving his potentially damaging testimony as well.

Still, shoulder to the wheel, he went on.

William Pearse, the man who ran the Bristol–Aquidneck Island ferry, testified that on December 20 he had ferried Avery over to the island at about two o'clock in the afternoon. He had met Avery once before, when bringing him over for yet another four-day meeting. Avery was not particularly talkative during their more recent trip but did ask about the location of the coal mines on the island. Pearse said they were on the west coast of the island, perhaps one mile south of where the ferry landed.

Definitely placing Avery's arrival on the island at two o'clock, Staples attempted to trace his movements from there. Peleg Cranston collected tolls at Howland's Ferry Bridge, a stone span that connected Aquidneck Island to Tiverton. He testified that on December 20, between two o'clock and three-thirty in the afternoon, a stranger in a black hat and surtout (a frock coat) stopped at the tollhouse, commented on the weather, paid his toll and crossed the bridge. The man had made some comment that led Cranston to believe he was bound for Fall River. The man in the hat was clearly in a hurry.

George Lawton was standing on his "piazza" about three o'clock when he saw a man in a broad-brimmed black hat cross the stone bridge, "walking very fast."

Ann (or Annis) Norton of Tiverton, who also lived near the bridge, likewise saw a man with "a hat rather a broad brim, which made me think it was a Methodist minister." She commented to her father, "If that man walks at that rate he will get to Ohio before night." A friend had once pointed Avery out to her on a trip to Bristol over the summer, and while she thought the fast-moving man in the big hat was "familiar," she could not swear it was Avery and expressed doubt that she would even recognize the man if she saw him again.

Two laborers, Benjamin Manchester and Abner Davis, were working in a field next to Durfee's stack yard that day, and toward sunset they saw a stranger in a broad-brimmed hat. The men were clearing the field of rocks and boulders, blowing the larger ones into more manageable pieces with kegs of black powder. Just as one rock was detonated, one of the men "sang out" to the stranger to beware of falling debris as he crossed the field. The man in the hat waited until it was safe before moving across the field, climbing over a wall and moving on north, toward Fall River.

John Durfee also remembered seeing the man the night before he found Sarah's body, though he had attributed no importance to it that night. The next morning, however, he must have wondered.

Manchester and Davis put their powder and tools away in a cart nearby and left it in the field overnight. They had several bags in which to store their equipment and also to use as cushions to sit on when drilling rocks. On Friday morning, shortly before Sarah's body was discovered, Davis noticed that one of the bags had been opened and its side was "unlaced." Having been among those who saw Sarah's corpse that morning, he stated in court that "the bags we set on to drill are sewed with the same kind of string" as that with which she was hanged.

At Lawton's tavern in Fall River, Margaret Hambly served supper to a tall man on the night of the twentieth. She was asked if she saw that man in the courtroom now. Looking from face to face, she sad she did not see the man there.

Someone, perhaps Bullock, pointed out Luke Drury, one of the court reporters, and asked her if he was the man she had seen

"Yes, that is the man," she said firmly. Lawyers and justices must have exchanged uneasy glances and annoyed smiles.

Avery and fellow minister Samuel Drake were requested to stand. The witness was asked if either of the two could be the man to whom she had served supper that night. She hesitatingly confessed that either one of them could be the one she had seen—yes, it was certainly one of them and not the first man she had identified.

Avery was pointed out to her. An awkward silence hung in the air and was broken by some stifled laughter, and the witness was dismissed.

Peleg Cranston, the tollkeeper, stated that he closed the gate every night at sundown. Apparently, the locked gate was not a serious obstacle, and it was easy to jump down off the bridge onto the beach and go around. Cranston testified that on the morning of Friday the twenty-first he found footprints in the sand leading around the gate. Someone had come to the island from Tiverton during the night. He added that he checked each morning and that it was not at all unusual to find such tracks.

About 9:30 p.m. on the evening of the twentieth, Avery banged loudly on the door of Jeremiah Gifford, who operated the ferry from the island to Bristol. He woke the ferryman up out of a sound sleep. Gifford had seen Avery land from Bristol earlier that day. The agitated Avery asked to cross back to Bristol immediately, but Gifford refused, saying it was too late. The minister insisted that it was not so late as he thought, adding that he must get home that night, as there was an illness in his family. According to later rumor, he offered to pay twice the usual fare. Still, Gifford would not bring him across and said that he could spend the night upstairs in a spare room and be ferried home in the morning.

Jane Gifford, the ferryman's daughter, found Avery alone in the kitchen early the next morning, warming himself by the stove.

"I did not know you were preaching on the island last night," she said, as she busied herself making a cake.

"I did not," he replied. "I was here on business of my own. At Brother Cook's."

Jane's brother rowed Avery back to Bristol a short time later.

Presiding Elder Abraham Merrill, Avery's superior in the church, came to see him one night at home during the hearing. Weary after long days in court, Avery still tried to make the older man welcome, even though a cloud now hung over his house.

They spoke for some time before Merrill, "with a heart apparently big with feeling," as Avery would later write, came to the point of his visit.

"Brother Avery, it is my duty to believe you innocent until you are proved guilty," his presiding elder said. "You know, and your God knows, whether you are guilty or not; but I charge you, as you will answer it at the dreadful tribunal of Heaven, not to add sin to sin. If you have disclosures to make, I do not ask you to make them to me, or to any of your brethren in the ministry; it would be too much for such to witness against you, which must be done; but to some other person. I must warn you not to add sin to sin. Don't do so, on your peril."

Clearly, Merrill had some doubts about his subordinate's involvement with Sarah Cornell. If he was indeed guilty of seducing her or even murdering her, he should not "add sin to sin" by trying to cover it up.

"Brother Merrill, Heaven is my witness, that I never desired to touch, and I never did, that woman, in any unlawful way."

This seemed to satisfy Merrill, and before he left, he assured Avery that he only wished to see the truth, whatever it might be, come to light.

Avery never took the stand in his own defense. After submitting his written statement on the first day, he remained enigmatically silent for the rest of the hearing. This is due to the vagaries of Rhode Island law at the time, which prohibited the accused from testifying. The case for the defense was puzzled together by others.

Reverend Drake, the man Avery summoned when Bidwell first brought the news from Tiverton, repeated what he had been told when he arrived at Avery's house.

Ephraim Avery arrived on the island about two o'clock and set off southward, in the direction of the coal mines, where he had been told he could find a good price on coal. It was unseasonably warm and not a bad day for a walk.

Nearing the mines, he saw a man with a gun and asked him if the mines were open for business. The man said no. A disappointed Avery changed plans, deciding instead to visit the Freeborns, a family he had met at a four-day meeting some time ago. They lived a short distance south of the mines, and Avery continued on this way down the west side of the island. Walking along country roads and occasionally hopping over stone walls and cutting through fields, Avery soon met a young boy driving a herd of sheep near the Freeborn home. He asked the boy if the family was home, but the boy said no and that the Freeborns were away for the day. Disappointment must now have become frustration, and instead of knocking on the Freeborns' door himself, Avery continued to the home of another Methodist, one sister Wilcox, who lived several miles farther down on the island.

Now it was getting dark, and as he made his way toward the home of sister Wilcox, he must have made one or more wrong turns. By the time he had gotten his bearings, he realized he was still quite a distance from the Wilcox house. Debating what to do and rubbing at his ankle, still stiff and sore after injuring it in Lowell over the summer, he decided to turn back to the ferry. He arrived too late to cross and, as Gifford had already testified, spent the night on Aquidneck Island.

The defense needed to establish that Avery had spent the day miles away from Tiverton and Durfee's stack yard. They were, however, seriously hobbled in their efforts by failing to locate either the man with the gun or the boy driving the sheep whom Avery claimed to have met. They could not establish a much-needed alibi.

Jane Gifford's testimony presented another problem. According to her, Avery claimed to be visiting a "Brother Cook" on the island, but his written statement made no mention of anyone named Cook. One of them, either the minister or the ferryman's daughter, must be wrong. The defense chose to handle this bluntly, by calling a string of witnesses to swear that Jane Gifford's "character for truth and veracity was bad." If her testimony would not alibi Avery, then she must be discredited. In fact, the witnesses called to speak against her had no other statements to make regarding the case; they had been brought in specifically to destroy her character and, thereby, her testimony as well. In retaliation, the prosecution put their own witnesses on the stand to assert that Jane was reliable, but the damage was done.

More testimony was called into question. According to William Pearse, who had been present in the sink room on Christmas Day when Orswell confronted Avery, the engineer had been much more tentative in making an identification at the time. Supposedly, Avery had quizzed Orswell—what color coat was the man wearing? Did he have a watch? A cane? Spectacles? After a barrage of questions, Orswell admitted at the time that he "should not like to swear" that the man before him was the same man who had handed him the letter. Pearse alleged that Orswell had been much less certain in the sink room than he had been in the courtroom.

To further damage Orswell's allegations, several ministers who attended the four-day meeting in Providence in November asserted that, while Avery had attended that meeting, he had been with them between nine and ten o'clock, when he was supposedly at the dock, handing the letter over to the engineer.

Sarah herself came under fire when the defense called witnesses to testify to her rocky past and occasionally erratic and emotional behavior. Former co-worker Lydia Pervere, brought down from Lowell, described her as "deranged at times, she would cry, scream, etc., came into the mill one day dressed all in white; went out and changed it. I took it to be craziness, artful, sly."

More stories were heard—that Sarah had refused to attend a camp meeting because Avery would be there; others said that she confessed "she was intimate with three young men."

Mary Anne Barnes, also of Lowell, reported that "once a young man carried her out in a chaise to a tavern; they went into a chamber, had wine, etc.," leaving no question as to what the "etc." entailed. To make matters worse, she asserted that this had happened on the Sabbath.

Attacks on her character continued, all in the same vein: "Her character bad—improper conduct—keeping unseasonable hours—unchaste—light—vain—said to be insane at times."

With Sarah's reputation ruined, the defense moved on to other matters.

One William Hamilton said that he stopped at the general store in Tiverton on the night of the twentieth to smoke a pipe and catch up on the news with the other menfolk. He left about quarter to nine, and when passing Durfee's farm he heard a "squall." At first he thought it might have been a cat, "but it altered and seemed like a human cry; three or four shrill cries as of a woman beaten; stopped about two minutes, it then sounded like stifled groans."

Reaching the top of the hill and looking around, no doubt badly startled by sudden cries in a cold and otherwise quiet night, he saw nothing and continued on his way home.

"My impression at the time was that it was a woman in distress," he said.

Using Hamilton's testimony to fix the time of Sarah's death between 8:45 and 9:00 p.m., the defense pointed out that it would have been impossible for Avery to walk from Durfee's stack yard to Gifford's ferry—a distance of some nine miles—in thirty or forty-five minutes, to arrive at about 9:30 p.m. No man could accomplish such an athletic feat, especially not one limping along on a bad ankle.

After two long weeks, the hearing drew to a close. Prosecution and defense made their closing statements, each highlighting the strongest points in their favor. Bullock deputized Randolph to handle the closing arguments, and he spoke "in an able and eloquent manner for three hours," according to contemporary accounts. It was obvious that Sarah Cornell, with her sad history and erratic behavior, was the unfortunate victim of her own profligate lifestyle. Avery had no hand in her death; indeed, he was a minister of the

Gospel and she a promiscuous slattern. Why would suspicion be leveled at a good man such as he?

Orswell's testimony had been proven false, at least to the satisfaction of the defense. The person who handed the letter to the engineer—whoever that might have been!—was the author of all the letters. The deceased's name had even been misspelled on the letters as *Connell* rather that *Cornell*—and surely, an educated man such as Avery would be able to spell her name correctly.

Finally, simply and most compelling of all, Sarah had committed suicide, an act, by its own awful nature, planned and carried out by her and her alone.

In his two-hour summation, lasting until 2:00 a.m. on Sunday, Staples contended that Sarah Maria Cornell did not die by her own hand and indeed could not have—she died by violence, by strangulation. But was Avery her murderer? The evidence of the letters, all clearly written by him, along with Orswell's testimony and his strange absence from home on the fateful night—Staples characterized Avery's account of his time on the island as "unreasonable and contradictory"—fitted together and strongly indicated his guilt. He had crossed Peleg Cranston's bridge into Tiverton, probably visited the site of the planned assignation, slipped into Fall River for a quick supper and then kept the fatal appointment with the hapless mill girl. When she passed out from the pain of his failed attempt at inducing an abortion, Avery saw only one way out: strangling her with a cord he found in the nearby cart and tying her body to a stake in the stack yard, hoping to make it look like a suicide.

The two tired justices of the peace adjourned the court. They would give their decision in twelve hours.

On Monday, January 7, at two o'clock in the afternoon, Bristol held its collective breath, and Justices Howe and Haile took their seats behind the bench and handed down their decision. Howe made a long statement in which he systematically demolished each piece of evidence and testimony that had been brought against Avery.

Sarah's body and the condition in which it was found clearly indicated that she had committed suicide. No one could identify the stranger seen near the scene as Avery, none of the letters was conclusively proved to be written by him and his spotless reputation trumped hers. Howe commented disapprovingly "that she appears to be addicted to almost every vice."

Haile echoed his fellow justice's thoughts, and together they ruled that there was not probable cause to suspect Ephraim K. Avery in the death of Sarah M. Cornell.

With a final bang of the gavel, the prisoner was set free.

Glaring around the courtroom at the crowd, the triumphant Nathaniel Bullock declared "that if the people of Tiverton and Fall River are not satisfied, Mr. Avery was then ready to enter into a recognizance for his appearance at the next term of the Supreme Court."

Bullock's gaze fell upon Colonel Harvey Harnden, a man who had been so active in building a case against the minister. Harnden reluctantly shook his head and said it was impossible—the court had decided there was no probable cause, and so there was nothing on which to enter into such a recognizance. Over the shouted questions and recriminations in the courtroom, he asked for a copy of the justices' decision to bring back to Fall River with him.

He obtained a copy a few days later and read it aloud to a meeting of some six hundred people back at the Lyceum, including of course members of the Committee of Vigilance. The outrage expressed by the assembled throng was predictable. The question was debated, and it was quickly decided that steps must be taken to obtain another warrant for Avery's arrest on suspicion of murder.

On Wednesday, January 9, the *Fall River Weekly Recorder* wrote:

> *We impeach not the motives of the gentlemen who composed the Court on this occasion in coming to the decision they have; but with the testimony which has been elicited in this case before them, we certainly are astonished—as we believe the citizens of this community generally are—at the conclusions arrived at. The evidence against Mr. Avery, it is true, was wholly circumstantial; but the intimate connexion between the different parts, forming altogether as a whole, such a distinct and perfect chain of testimony, as in our opinion, must have been very difficult if not impossible to resist. But the verdict of acquittal has gone forth to the public. Then we say, let the whole facts in the case go forth too. Let them be circulated far and wide; and let the voice of the community be the test whether that verdict is a righteous one.*

Harnden spent the next few days consulting lawyers, sheriffs and even the Rhode Island attorney general, finally obtaining an arrest warrant on January 11. He handed it over to Deputy Sheriff Paul, who had arrested Avery just a few weeks before. Paul moved to serve the warrant.

But Ephraim Avery was nowhere to be found.

CHAPTER 8

"Absconded from Bristol"

On January 14, the *Providence Journal* wrote:

The Daily Advertiser and American of Saturday evening says: "We learn from a most unquestionable source that the Rev. Mr. Avery has absconded from Bristol." We have heard it stated that this report was promulgated by the Sheriff, who has been deputed from Newport County to arrest him, for examination, and if need should be, for trial.

Rumors flew carelessly in the wake of the minister's disappearance. His wife and family, left on their own, weren't saying anything, which of course gave rumormongers free rein. Some insisted that he had gone into hiding somewhere among the Methodists, while others thought he must have been sheltered by prominent citizens of Bristol who had attended the hearing. There was even vague talk that he had fled to Cuba.

Harvey Harnden, ever the hard-nosed man of action, rose to the challenge before him and spent a couple of days making inquiries and following up leads, visiting taverns and questioning toll collectors. He soon established that Avery had indeed fled Bristol and was heading north.

Five days later, on January 21, after sleeplessly traveling icy New England roads from town to town and interviewing numerous civilians and government officials, Harnden traced his quarry to the small town of Rindge, New Hampshire.

He found that three or four years before, a woman named Mayo had been brought up on charges before the Methodist congregation to which she belonged (the Methodists seemed to do little else other than hold four-day meetings and bring one another up on charges in the old days), and her husband, Captain Mayo, sent for Avery to plead her case. Avery successfully defended her against the (unspecified) charges and she remained a member in regular standing. Captain Mayo and his wife now lived in Rindge, and Harden's informant, a local baker he enlisted to gather intelligence for him, commented, "You know, one good turn deserves another."

Harnden was now convinced that Avery was hiding in the Mayo home.

Assembling several local men, including a deputy sheriff, and commandeering the baker's sleigh, Harnden swung into action. Assuring them that he "would do all the talking and fighting if any should be necessary," he positioned the men outside the house to observe the doors and windows while he and the deputy sheriff burst into the home.

Three people sat around a fire in the front room: the Mayos and a local Methodist minister.

Harnden demanded to see Ephraim K. Avery.

"Ephraim K. Avery…?" Captain Mayo asked thoughtfully. "Ephraim K. Avery? I never heard of any such man."

The minister, sitting in the opposite corner, wondered aloud if there hadn't been a minister in Lowell named Avery. Captain Mayo shook his head and again declared that he had never heard of anyone by that name. Having no time for such games, Harnden ordered that they produce him at once, and if they did not, he would search the house until he found him.

While her husband continued to deny all knowledge of Avery, Mrs. Mayo slipped quietly out of the room. One of the men outside tapped on the window and told Harnden that he had seen her go upstairs and knock on a door at the head of the stairs. He heard her call Avery's name. Apparently, Harnden had chosen an assistant with superhuman hearing.

Seizing a candle, Harnden bounded up the steps and pushed past the startled Mrs. Mayo and into the room. A low fire burned in the fireplace. On a table stood a recently extinguished candle; the wick still glowed and a curl of smoke trailed upward. There was a bed in the room, still warm and "tumbled." Folded blankets covered the windows, and Harden noted a stack of wood for the fire, some cooking and eating utensils and even several pies. "I thought a man might make himself very comfortable in the room if he could submit to the confinement," he later wrote.

Behind him, an angry Mrs. Mayo said he was after innocent blood. Without ceasing his search for a moment, Harnden shot back that he was not after innocent blood, he was after Ephraim Avery.

An 1890s photo of the Newport County Jail, little changed from the time Avery spent there. *Courtesy Providence Public Library.*

He found the minister hiding behind the door. Harnden thrust out a hand and asked, "Mr. Avery, how do you do?"

Avery choked and steadied himself against the wall. In the two weeks since Harnden had last seen him, Avery had grown a full beard, which substantially changed his appearance—just what might be expected from a man on the run.

"I suppose you cannot legally take me from this state without a warrant from the Governor," the shaken Avery finally blurted out.

The cautious, by-the-book Harnden had diligently obtained the required paperwork every step of the way, and produced the appropriate documents. Avery surrendered himself to Harnden's custody and was marched out of the house, straight past the now silent Captain Mayo. They started back for Rhode Island that night.

Reaching Boston, the exhausted Harnden and his prisoner were thronged with curious visitors. Perhaps motivated by caution and perhaps by a kind of compassion, Harnden refused admission to all but those who Avery himself wished to see. This would be repeated at every stop along their journey, as word spread and interest grew. Whenever they stopped to water the horses or eat a quick meal, the curious came to see. If they expected to see Avery in irons, and no doubt many of them did, they were disappointed, as Harnden felt such drastic and meretricious steps were unnecessary. As they pulled into Fall River, Avery perhaps justifiably feared that "in consequence of the very great excitement in that village, he would be taken by the populace and torn in pieces."

But he was not, and on Friday, January 25, 1833, he was handed over to the authorities at Tiverton at ten o'clock in the morning. A brief hearing was held—records of which do not survive—and he was then sent to the Newport County Jail.

In 1833, murder was a capital offense. If found guilty, he would suffer the same fate as it seemed had befallen Sarah Cornell—death by hanging. The irony was probably lost on no one.

The Newport jail was built about 1772, replacing an earlier one on the same site, and it served more as a temporary place to hold inmates rather than a long-term prison. It was never especially secure and had seen some escapes over the years, but it was more than enough to confine Reverend Avery. He was locked into a cell with a narrow window, and the bed was merely a straw-stuffed sack and a couple of moth-eaten blankets. He got no sleep that first night, kept awake by the cold as "the grating sound of bars of iron and the turning of keys and the retiring footsteps of the jailor died away on my ear."

He paced his cell all night, probably only pausing to pray, his mind racing back and forth between thoughts of the cross and the noose.

CHAPTER 9

"Say Nothing to No One"

In the months leading up to the trial, the *Fall River Weekly Reporter* got its wish—the facts did go forth to the public, often mixed with a large amount of rumor.

The last week of January, Sarah's body was once more exhumed and autopsied by Drs. Wilbur and Hooper. Little had changed, aside from a white mold now covering her face and some of the incisions from their previous exam. Turning their attention to the livid bruises, "to determine whether the livid appearances abovementioned were caused by bruises or putrefaction, we tried the test of washing, as laid down in books." Results were mixed, with some of the areas tested washing clean and others not, indicating that some of the lividity was from bruising and some from putrefaction.

Arriving to testify at the Bristol hearing, Sarah's brother-in-law, Grindall Rawson, had in hand a letter that she had written one month before her death. He had not been allowed to submit it to the court, so he submitted it instead to the newspapers. Thanks to the scissors-and-paste approach to journalism, the letter was soon reprinted in a number of papers:

> *Fall River, Nov. 18th, 1832.*
>
> *Dear Friends—I had been looking for a letter from you, but began to think you had almost forgotten me, when I went to the office and found one from you, enclosing one from my own brother, and also one from E.K. Avery at the same time. He came to Fall River as I wrote you, but did not come until Friday, and staid over the Sabbath. I could not well avoid*

him. I went to the meetings in the evening. On Friday evening I went, and when I got there, Mr. Avery was at prayer. I staid and heard him preach, as I concluded I would see him. After meeting was closed I spoke to him. I told him I wished to see him, he seemed to decline, there were so many round. I told him if I did not see him there, I should come to Bristol; he however stopped and we talked five minutes, promised to come and see me the next evening. He came and I spent an hour with him. He said as I told he would, that if that was my case it was not his, and said I must go to a doctor immediately; said he had burned my letters—if he had have known what would have happened he would have kept them—said I must never swear it, for if that was my case he would take care of me—spoke very feelingly of his wife and children—said I must say it belonged to a man that was dead, for, said he, I am dead to you—that is I cannot marry you. He owned and denied it two or three times. He left me by saying I might wait a few weeks and then I might write to him. I pledged him my word and honor I would not expose him if he would settle it—therefore you must not mention his name to any one. If it should come out, you can say it belonged to a Methodist minister, but that we settled it, and that I do not choose to tell whose it is. I wrote to him last week informing him my fears. I told him he must not deny it, if he did I should expose him immediately. I have received the following answer without any name.

Nov. 13th, 1832.

Miss Cornell—I have just received your letter with no small surprise, and will say in reply, I will do all you ask, only keep it secret. I wish you to write me as soon as you get this, naming some time and place where I can see you, and wait for my answer before I come, and I will say whether it is convenient or not. I will keep your letter till I see you, and wish you to keep mine, and have them when I see you. Write soon—say nothing to no one. Yours in haste.

I suppose he wishes me to return his letter, therefore I have copied it, as I ought to presume, as James says, that my friends will not expose it for my sake. I have written to him again, and am expecting an answer every day. What the result will be, I know not. I still have hopes and fears. I do not, however, wish you to do any thing for me till I send you word. There is a girl here that has had a child, and went into the factory again in six weeks—She gets her child boarded for fifty cents a week. It will not make half the noise here that it would in the country. I lost eleven days in the month of October, *and just cleared my board. I have since made about nine or ten shillings per week clear. Shall try to save six dollars a month this winter— and that is as much as I can do if I am as well as I have been a month past. I shall try to work till the first of March. The girls make from three to four dollars per week in the summer, but the days are short and the water is low now. We can't do very much. I have never been out of money yet, and don't think I shall be very soon. I wish you to take care of my things if you don't see me this dozen years and when I send for them I want you to send them, and not before. I do not want for any thing at present. I have kept at home except on the Sabbath, but the Methodists begin to know me and say, good morning sister, as I go to the factory. I am glad that you have plenty of work. I hope you will get along for help. Mr. Rawson, your good friend Graham did not meet with so good reception in Fall River as he expected. The people were not much pleased with him, he extolled himself too much, and money was at the bottom. He wanted ten dollars a night, and could not get it, and so he left the place. Mr. Fowler has got an elegant meeting-house just completed. It is to be dedicated next week. I have never heard him preach—I can't get time. I don't know but I shall go to the dedication. I don't know as I have any more to write. I shall inform you if any thing new takes place, and you must not forget you have a sister in Fall River. My love to my mother. You must burn this letter. Farewell. Your sister, SARAH M. CORNELL.*

Clearly, this is a damning letter. It speaks quite openly of Sarah's relationship with Avery, his reception of the news of her pregnancy and her plans to quietly give birth. She was obviously not in a suicidal frame of mind, as she was concerned over money and had been looking into how other women in her situation handled matters, such as the cost of boarding the child and how soon she might be able to return to work. Sarah was looking toward her future.

Shortly after this letter was sent, Sarah moved from Mrs. Cole's to the Hathaway boardinghouse. The days of missed work referred to are probably due to morning sickness, and Sarah knew that soon her pregnancy would begin to show, so she may have chosen the smaller, more secluded Hathaway house and "kept at home" to avoid the shaking of judgmental heads.

The defense could not allow this letter to be read in the courtroom; they must have acted preemptively to ensure that it would never even make it to open court. In any event, it was so thoroughly quashed that it is not even mentioned in the court transcripts. But due to Grindall Rawson's actions, it would be seen by untold thousands of newspaper readers.

One failing on the part of the defense was its inability to alibi Avery on the fatal evening. The missing seven and a half hours gave him ample time to do exactly what the prosecution accused him of—arrive on the island, cross over to Tiverton via Peleg Cranston's bridge, enter Fall River under cover of darkness, eat a quick meal at Lawton's tavern, commit the crime and make it to Gifford's by approximately 9:30 p.m.

Reverend Drake, a Methodist minister on the island and the first man Avery had called for upon hearing he was suspected in Sarah's death, had canvassed the island looking for witnesses who could help alibi Avery but came up empty-handed. Despite his best efforts, he could locate no one who could testify to seeing Avery on the west side of the island that day, and he could find neither the man with the gun nor the boy driving the sheep.

But he did find Sarah Jones.

Sarah Jones was a forty-year-old woman who lived near the coal mines that Avery spoke of. Late in the morning of December 20, she had seen an unfamiliar man pass by her house and go through a nearby gate. Hearing this, Drake arranged to have her brought to Bristol to be interviewed by Avery and Nathaniel Bullock at the minister's home.

Sarah explained a little embarrassedly that she didn't quite understand how she could help, as she had seen the stranger between eleven o'clock and noon, at least two hours before Avery arrived on the island. Clearly, this man was someone else. But the minister and his attorney would not give up so easily.

Bullock spent some time sketching out a map of the island in chalk on the kitchen floor, occasionally asking questions to clarify points of geography. Once he was done and the lay of the land established, he asked Avery what color the gate by Sarah's house was, and he correctly identified it as white, lending at least some credence to the fact that he had been the man in question.

Bullock asked if his client resembled the man.

Sarah Jones said he might, but she couldn't be quite sure. She had been in her house when he passed, so Avery went outside and walked up and down the street several times while she watched. Again, she couldn't be certain—he looked something like the man, but was too tall. And besides, she saw the man before Avery even boarded the ferry. She apologized and rose to go.

Bullock pressed her. "Are you sure it was in the forenoon? Couldn't it just as easily have been in the afternoon?"

Sarah stood firm.

After several failed attempts to get her to change her mind, Avery stopped her as she was leaving and laid a hand upon her shoulder.

"My life is worth a thousand worlds to me," he implored. "And my life depends on my evidence." And then he asked her to keep their discussion secret.

Drake made one more attempt to convince her on the way back to Pearse's ferry, asking why it was not just as easy for her to say it was the afternoon.

"Because it is not so," she replied.

"What reason do you have for thinking so?"

"Because I know the forenoon from the afternoon," was her exasperated response.

At the Bristol hearing, she had been called by the defense to testify to seeing a man fitting Reverend Avery's description near the coal mine on the afternoon of the twentieth. When she insisted she saw the man in the morning and could not be convinced to change her mind, she was quickly and embarrassedly dismissed.

Stories depicting Avery as an angry, vengeful man began to surface.

When stationed in Scituate, Massachusetts, a coastal town south of Boston, Avery had crossed swords with Fanny Winsor, a prominent and popular member of the Methodist congregation there. For unknown reasons, he took an almost immediate dislike to her—perhaps he felt threatened by her popularity, perhaps it was a clash of personalities and perhaps it was something else altogether. We know the result of their conflict, even if we do not know its cause.

Loathing each other cordially, they were still forced to endure at least a certain amount of time together. When discussing a "somewhat intemperate" parishioner who had recently lost his wife, Avery callously commented to Fanny that the fellow would "soon drown his sorrows." When she repeated this to the bereaved man—who happened to be her uncle—things became openly hostile.

Avery took steps to have Fanny Winsor read out of the church, accusing her of several kinds of unchristian behavior. His attempts failed, as the congregation sided with her and even issued her a certificate of good standing. The next few months must have passed uncomfortably and awkwardly for all involved until Avery received his new assignment, to Saugus, a town to the north of Boston. But he also ran into difficulties there and ended up in court for the first time.

Avery was invited to occasionally preach before the local Congregationalists, who lacked a minister of their own. They also invited a Reverend Norris to preach at other times when Avery was unavailable. Avery didn't like Norris any more than he had liked Fanny Winsor. Again, the motive is not entirely clear. It may have been a simple personal antagonism, he may have worried that the Congregationalists would prefer Norris over him or it may have been that Norris was a member of the Reformed Methodist Church, a group that had split off from the Methodist Episcopal Church, to which Avery belonged. Regardless, the tension between the two was noticeable.

Avery delivered a few fiery sermons in which he warned the Congregationalists to beware Reverend Norris. He maintained that the other minister was a liar and a thief, even asserting that once, when employed in a glassware business, Norris had pilfered numerous items to bring home for his own table.

Norris sued for defamation of character and won. Avery appealed, and then settled, paying $190 in damages, a sizeable sum in those days.

Abraham Merrill, Avery's presiding elder, had attended the trial at Saugus. When he later appeared at the Bristol hearing and testified that he knew of nothing that counted against Avery's character, Norris was irate. He made sure that the story of his legal tangle with Avery was heard, even mailing out letters and pamphlets detailing the case. He made it clear that he pitied Avery more than he scorned him, but one wonders.

Other, more colorful rumors began to spread.

Of course Avery had been released by the Bristol court, some muttered; Haile, Howe and Avery were all Freemasons, and the justices would not condemn a brother Mason. Others contended that the Methodist church had simply bought off the court; with Rhode Island's long history of corruption (the state was disparagingly called "Rogue's Island" for a long time), this did not seem impossible.

It was said that Avery had spent ten years as a pirate on the Spanish main—perhaps this was somehow related to the speculations that he had fled to Cuba after the Bristol hearing. It was also whispered that he had a wife who had died under mysterious circumstances years before; perhaps Sarah Cornell was not his only victim!

As titillating and pleasingly suggestive as these rumors are, none of them was backed by anything resembling evidence.

Some stories filtered down from Lowell. The house in which he lived during his assignment there had a study located in a remote corner of the building, far away from the bedrooms of the rest of the family. Perfect, it was said, for sneaking young girls in and out without anyone knowing. Those who heard about this must have nodded knowingly when it was further revealed that this infamous study also contained a bed.

Reportedly, Avery's son, far too young to fully understand the import of what he was saying, had several times innocently repeated, "I saw Pa kiss Sarah Maria Cornell on the road." One supposes he was quickly hushed by his elders.

Of course, as with any high-profile case, this one attracted the attention of some who were simply overeager and some who were probably just lunatics. Harvey Harnden received a few letters from people who claimed to have encountered a heavily disguised Avery, including one asserting that he had visited a doctor to inquire about inducing an abortion.

In February, Harnden published a thirty-six-page pamphlet detailing his pursuit and capture of the errant minister. The thirteen thousand copies sold well. While he was tracking his quarry through New England, the Rhode Island state legislature offered a reward "not to exceed $300" for Avery's capture. When Harnden applied for the reward after his return, the frugal legislators paid him $250.

Also in February, Avery received a bizarre letter at the jail:

> *Providence, Feb. 17, 1833*
> *Rev. E.K. Avery—*
> *You are accused of the willful murder S.M. Cornell, and in a few days will have your trial for that crime. Whether you are really guilty or innocent, the public opinion is almost unanimous against you. It may be supposed by a few, that positive proof is requisite to induce a jury in this state to convict a person of premeditated murder; but circumstantial evidence, when perfectly concurring in all its parts, and when abundant, too, is and must appear to a jury to be stronger and more certain, than scanty positive proof. Such a chain as that of corroborating testimony is prepared against you; but notwithstanding this fact, strange as it may seem, I believe you not guilty of the horrible crime alleged against you. So thinking, I am inclined to counsel you for your acquittal of this charge, not only by the jury, but also in a great measure by public opinion. You no doubt are surprised at this communication; but it's scarcely more unexpected to you, than was to me*

Another illustration from *The Terrible Hay Stack Murder*, depicting the rumor of a disguised Avery being seen on the night of Sarah's death. *Courtesy Brown University.*

the change in my own opinion of your guilt; and were I not a physician, I probably should not now have changed my mind, or have discovered a clew by which to acquit you. This aid I am ready to give you; but as I believe it to be by far the most important to you of any counsel you will get, so I shall hold it for a fee. The trifling sum of fifty dollars must be deposited with some one, who, in case you avail yourself of the suggestion I may give you, or your counsel for you, and you shall be acquitted, will give on the day of your acquittal the strictly confidential between your counsel, the gentleman who has the money in trust, and ourselves.

Should you think proper to accept of this proposition, you will cause to be inserted in the editorial column of the Newport Mercury of the 23d inst. the following—"A physician's proposition is complied with." You will then immediately hear from me.

Respectfully, &c.

He does not seem to have responded.

CHAPTER 10

"God Send You a Good Deliverance"

The grand jury indicted Avery for murder on March 8. Up to the last moment, he was convinced they would set him free. The trial was scheduled to commence on May 6. He had already been in the Newport County Jail for one month; now he had two more to wait alone in his cell.

Things improved for him somewhat. Randolph, one member of his legal team, and a Mr. Kent, another benefactor, each brought him a bed. Randolph also supplied a stove and fuel to keep him warm. The jailor and his wife, he later wrote, "at times felt tender toward me" and gave him "a Bible, Bible Dictionary, and a few other volumes to read…I spent my time in reading, meditating, and prayer."

Life went on outside the jail walls. President Andrew Jackson, now serving his second term, managed to settle the ugly Nullification Crisis—wherein the recalcitrant South Carolina legislature refused to enforce a heavy federal tariff—without sending in troops, as he had threatened. Jackson then moved on to vetoing the renewal of the Second Bank of the United States, touching off the bank war with his hated banker rival Nicholas Biddle. The Trail of Tears continued, as Indian tribes were forced westward. Closer to home, Connecticut teacher Prudence Crandall made headlines when she began accepting "colored" students. She would be arrested later that summer.

As Avery's trial drew near, the press descended on Newport. Reporters from Boston, New York and Philadelphia arrived with notebooks and pencils in hand to ensure that curious readers would know exactly what was happening in the Rhode Island courtroom.

Newport's Old Colony House, completed in 1741, where Avery's murder trial was held. *Courtesy Newport Historical Society.*

Today, Newport is remembered either as a leading city in the colonial period or as the gilded playground of fin de siècle robber barons. The 1830s were the trough between these two crests, and Newport was simply yet another worn-out New England seaport. Arriving in Newport the year before, at the beginning of the tour that would lead to *Democracy in America*, Alexis de Tocqueville described it in a letter home as "a collection of small houses, the size of chicken coops, but distinguished by a cleanness that is a pleasure to see and that we have no conception of in France." His traveling companion, Beaumont, was more descriptive:

> *We wandered about the town. It has 16,000 inhabitants, a magnificent harbor, newly fortified, tiny houses…so clean they resemble opera scenery. They are all painted. There is also a church whose bell tower is in a rather remarkable architectural style. I sketched it on Jules' album. We had been told that the women of Newport were noteworthy for their beauty; we found them extraordinarily ugly. This new race of people we saw bears no clear mark of its origin; it's neither English, nor French, nor German; it's mixture of all the nations. This race is entirely commercial. In the small city of Newport there are 4 or 5 banks; the same is true in all the cities in the Union.*

Several of the reporters who arrived in town for the trial are particularly noteworthy, as they would publish some of the fullest accounts of the proceedings. Benjamin Franklin Hallett was a graduate of Brown University, where he had studied law, who now worked as journalist for the *Boston Daily Advertiser*. Richard Hildreth, a Harvard graduate, was co-founder and editor of the *Boston Atlas*, established just the year before. Their accounts of the trial would soon be reprinted in book form and are still the main sources on which historians of the case rely.

Also worth particular mention was Richard Adams Locke, court reporter for the *New York Sun*. The British-born, Cambridge-educated Locke would produce a concise yet thorough account of the trial. He would later achieve infamy as the author of "The Great Moon Hoax," a series of articles that ran in the *New York Sun* in 1835, describing the "discovery" of life on the moon, including unicorns, bison and man-bats. Readers interested in knowing more about him, the Moon Hoax and the state of journalism in the 1830s should treat themselves to a copy of Matthew Goodman's *The Sun and the Moon: The Remarkable True Account of Hoaxers, Showmen, Dueling Journalists, and Lunar Man-Bats in Nineteenth-Century New York*.

It should be noted that the three accounts produced by these men reflect their own biases, as they highlight this piece of evidence and gloss over that piece of testimony. Hallett seems sympathetic to the prosecution, and

The Old Colony House still stands at the head of Washington Square in downtown Newport. *Photo by Robert O'Brien.*

Hildreth leans toward the defense; Locke likewise favors the defense, and his editorial comments and often wry remarks make for amusing reading.

The attorneys on the case were no less interesting. Albert Collins Greene was the forty-one-year-old attorney general leading the prosecution, with several other lawyers working under him, including William Staples, who had prosecuted during the Bristol hearing. Defending was Yale graduate Jeremiah Mason. At sixty-five years of age, he was a prominent Boston lawyer, a former New Hampshire politician and a good friend of Daniel Webster. He was well known as a formidable opponent.

Chief Justice Samuel Eddy, age sixty-four, a Brown graduate and former representative for Rhode Island, sat at the bench, with two other justices under him.

The trial opened on the morning of Monday, May 6, 1833, at ten o'clock. The courtroom was packed, and those who could not squeeze their way in stood outside, listening at the open windows. Avery entered the room with his legal team. The minister plainly showed the effects of his long confinement; Richard Adams Locke described him as "attenuated" and even "cadaverous." His clothes hung on him, and he wore purple spectacles; one wonders if he was hiding tired, bloodshot eyes behind the lenses.

The clerk of the court read the indictment. There were three charges, variations on a theme, that Avery—"Not having the fear of God before his eyes, but being moved and seduced by the instigation of the devil"—first, strangled Sarah Cornell with a cord, second, that he strangled her and hanged her from a stake, and third, that he beat her and strangled her.

"How say you, prisoner?" the clerk demanded. "Guilty or not guilty?"

"Not guilty, sir!" he declared.

"How will you be tried?"

"By God and my country," Avery said reverently.

"God send you a good deliverance."

Empanelling the jury took two days. Approximately 122 men were called and questioned, each being asked: "Are you related to either the prisoner or the deceased?" and "Have you any conscientious scruples to finding a man guilty of a crime punishable by death?" and "Have you formed or expressed any opinion of the guilt or innocence of the prisoner?"

With the jury selected, the clerk announced, "To this indictment the prisoner had pleaded not guilty, and for trial put himself upon God and his country—which country, gentlemen, you are! Hear the evidence!"

The minister attacks the mill girl in *The Terrible Hay Stack Murder. Courtesy Brown University.*

Much to the chagrin of the hungry reporters, Justice Eddy ordered a press blackout—no reports of the trial were to be published while the case was being heard. Once the case had been decided, they could publish whatever they saw fit. But until then, they must wait.

Greene had Dutee Pearce, one of the other lawyers on the team, make the opening statement. Pearce outlined the case for murder, saying that "every feeling that is cruel and mean, disgusting and relentless must have united in horrible energy."

In many ways, the Bristol hearing had been a dress rehearsal for the Newport trial. Most of the same witnesses were called to repeat much the same evidence. John Durfee described his discovery of the body and his subsequent actions; Elihu Hicks (whom Locke described as "an old man of irritable temperament and rather deaf") discussed the results of his inquest, whereupon he put on his hat and asked if he should be needed again; Orswell went over the story of the man who handed him the letter and the ninepence, clearly having been coached to be more emphatic about the identification to ward off the defense's inevitable challenges.

Richard Randolph cross-examined Dr. Wilbur after he testified to Sarah's seeking his medical opinion and his later examination of her dead body. "After a multitude of unimportant questions," according to Locke, Randolph inquired of the doctor, "Was there anything apparent from which you would swear, in a case of life and death, that a hard instrument had been introduced for the purpose of inducing an abortion?"

Probably echoing the thoughts of so many involved in the case, Wilbur replied, "There is a difference in feeling certain of a thing and being able to swear to it." Still, he felt that the bruising on Sarah's lower abdomen "could not have arisen from any other cause."

Dorcas Ford, one of the matrons who had examined Sarah's body, was questioned and then, upon cross-examination, Randolph asked, "Did you give your opinion at Bristol you thought she had been violated?"

"I said she had been dreadfully abused," Dorcas replied. "And I think so still!"

"What did you say at Bristol? Did you not say you thought she had been forced?"

"I was asked if there had been an attempt to produce abortion, and I said no. My opinion is she had been dreadfully abused."

"I wish to know if you swear it was an attempt to force her?"

"I think she was abused."

"Do you think she was violated?" Randolph asked again. "I wish you to answer that question."

"I repeat it, I think she was dreadfully abused."

"In what way?"

"Does not the bruise indicate abuse?" she asked incredulously.

Randolph turned to Greene for help; enlisting the aid of the prosecution showed how desperate he was.

"Did you mean that she had been forced?" Greene asked.

"I meant she had been abused."

"Did you believe there had been an attempt by any man at violent connection?"

"I suppose her life was forced from her, and you must judge in what way yourselves."

Eddy stepped in, asking the question himself and receiving the same answer. Randolph tried again and was told, "I shall give no other answer than I have."

"The witness says she shall give no other answer, and as I have only two courses to pursue, to move to commit her [hold her in contempt of court], or let her go," the frustrated Randolph fumed. "As she is a woman, I prefer the latter."

Dorcas was dismissed and took her seat.

Eleanor Owen was a Welsh woman who had settled in Tiverton. She described hearing screams about seven-thirty on the night of the twentieth, a good ninety minutes before William Hamilton heard his "squalls." This may have been an attempt to move the time of death back, giving Avery nearly two hours—ample time—to make the nine-mile journey from Durfee's stack yard to Gifford's ferry. Or it may have been meant to add credence to the theory that Avery had attempted to induce an abortion, resorting to murder when it failed.

Whatever Greene hoped to prove, he failed. Eleanor was a native speaker of Welsh, and her English was poor. She stumbled her way through her testimony, confusing the jury, and finally sighed as she said, "I can explain better in my language than yours." She was dismissed without a cross-examination.

Further attempts were made at establishing a timetable. Philip Bennett testified that he and Benjamin Manchester, one of the laborers who had been blowing up rocks and who later found part of Sarah's comb, walked from the stack yard to Gifford's in one hour and twenty-nine minutes. They mostly kept to the roads but did eventually cut through some fields and "trotted, but I did not at all fatigue myself."

Under cross-examination, he revealed that he and some others had been debating how long it might have taken Avery to get from one place to the other, and Dr. Hooper offered to pay three dollars if Bennett would make the journey and establish a time.

Lucretia Rawson, Sarah's sister, said that during the previous summer when Sarah stayed with the Rawsons, "I did her washing. I have means to know that eight days before the Thompson camp meeting she was unwell as women are once a month." Sarah left for Fall River in early October, and Lucretia (who is also occasionally referred to as Nancy for some strange reason) testified, "Before she left, the month came round but she did not have her turn…she told me what she feared might be her situation."

Greene then called Lucretia's husband, Grindall, who was in many ways the star witness for the prosecution. His story, it was hoped, would provide the final links in the chain between Sarah and Avery.

Rawson related how Sarah had visited the family, arriving in June and then going to work in his tailoring shop several weeks later. Sarah was eager to attend the camp meeting at Thompson, so Rawson arranged for an apprentice to bring her there and pick her up again a few days later. Being himself a Presbyterian, he had no interest in going.

On a Thursday afternoon during the meeting, Sarah said she encountered Avery. Taking a deep breath and screwing up her courage, she approached and said she wished to speak with him. He looked around and told her he would meet her later, when the horn sounded, signaling the commencement of the fiery preaching for which camp meetings were known.

When they met, Avery said it was too crowded to talk where they were and sent her off into the woods. She went, and a few minutes later he approached from another direction. They walked together deeper into the forest, farther and farther away from the crowds.

He asked her to remove her green spectacles and sit down.

"Have you burned the letters I sent you?" she asked, referring to the confessions she had sent him in Lowell.

"No," he replied. He still had them in a desk drawer in Bristol.

"You must burn them," she said firmly.

"I will burn them and settle the matter…on one condition."

Avery took her hand and laid his hand on her bosom.

Sarah was now in an awful quandary. She could give in to his demands and he would burn the letters, or she could refuse and he would still have something to hold over her. And if she refused…he was a beefy, six-foot-tall man, she was five feet tall, just over one hundred pounds and they were in a

Keeping a tryst in the woods at the Thompson camp meeting. *Courtesy Brown University.*

secluded part of the woods far away from the campground. Faced with a choice that was no choice at all, she gave in to him, probably closing her eyes and just waiting for it to be over. She may not have been forced, but she was certainly coerced.

Avery, buttoning up after, said over his shoulder that he would burn the letters upon his return to Bristol and left Sarah there among the trees.

A few weeks later, Sarah realized she was pregnant and confided in her sister, who in turn told her husband. After consulting with their minister (coincidentally also named Cornell, but not related) and their lawyer, Sarah chose to move to Fall River, partially to be nearer to Avery and partially because they were told that Massachusetts law was (in some unspecified way) more favorable to unwed mothers.

Certainly, Lucretia Rawson could have told the same story, especially as Sarah had come to her first. But Greene probably felt that the tale carried greater weight coming from the male head of the household than it would from the deceased's sister.

Avery visited Bidwell in October for a four-day meeting, and we know from the letter Rawson published that he met with Sarah at the time. Several witnesses were produced who testified to seeing a tall man and a short woman talking together in Fall River on October 20. One woman knew Sarah and identified her.

Zeruiah Hambley, a "rather young woman" according to Hallett, stated that in Tiverton, on the night of December 20, at about 7:00 p.m. she saw a tall man and a short woman walking arm in arm down the lane that led past the home of Eleanor Owen, the Welsh woman who heard screams at about 7:30 p.m. The short woman had on a cloak, and the tall man wore some kind of coat, but what kind, Zeruiah could not be sure.

Nancy Gladding of Bristol testified that on Tuesday, December 18, she had invited Avery to tea at her house on the following Thursday, December 20. The minister said he could come Friday instead, "for on Thursday we cannot so well come." Evidently, he already had plans for Thursday. But he visited on Friday, and there was nothing unusual in his behavior: "He was as cheerful and social as usual, made a prayer before he went, and his whole deportment was that of a Christian and a gentleman."

The prosecution rested, and Greene took his seat. Over the last six days, he and his team had made their case, connecting Avery to Sarah Cornell, exploring his motive for murder and, with Zeruiah Hambley's testimony, gotten as close as he could to actually placing the accused and the victim at the scene together. He had even, over the defense's strenuous objections,

The downstairs courtroom of the Old Colony House, which was thronged with reporters, witnesses and curious spectators during the trial. *Courtesy Newport Historical Society.*

gotten the pink letter (delivered by Orswell) admitted as material evidence that had been traced from the accused to the deceased, even though it had not been shown that Avery wrote it or even knew of its contents. Still, he had gotten the letter in, and the jury would draw its own conclusions, no matter what the judge said. He had also gotten the white letter (supposedly written in Smith's store) and the penciled note from the bandbox admitted.

He breathed a tired sigh, mopped the sweat from his brow and braced for the defense's response.

CHAPTER 11

"ALL THIS LOOKS LIKE DESIGN—LIKE CONSPIRACY"

Much was made at the time (and has been since) about a supposed vast and dark Methodist conspiracy to secure Avery's acquittal. True, members of the church were active in his defense, even raising some $6,000—a sizeable amount in those days—to help pay his legal fees. Ministers and members also aided in finding favorable witnesses and casting aspersions on unsympathetic ones. But it is not clear to what extent this constitutes a conspiracy on the part of the Methodist Episcopal Church, just as it is equally unclear when any group of people acting together to achieve a particular end crosses a line into "conspiracy." The Methodists may have simply been vigorously defending one of their own.

If you were accused of a crime, wouldn't you expect your friends, family and co-workers to come to your assistance? Would that be a conspiracy? To those on the opposing side of the question, it might be easy to say so.

Still, there were some highly questionable actions taken by those working to establish Avery's innocence, not limited to Bullock's witness tampering with Sarah Jones.

Attorney General Greene had dispatched Deputy Howland to bring a witness, known only as "Mrs. B.," from Tiverton to Newport to testify against Avery. The nature of her testimony is, unfortunately, nowhere recorded. Howland set off to get the witness. The defense must have seen the woman's name on the witness list, or acquired her name in some other way, and a Methodist clergyman (also unnamed) was sent racing down the roads in a frantic attempt to arrive ahead of the deputy.

He did, and when Howland appeared a few minutes later, he was informed that Mrs. B. was upstairs in bed, having been felled by a sudden and serious illness. She could see no one, and of course, under no circumstances could she even leave the house.

Probably rolling his eyes at the charade, Howland returned to the court for a writ of attachment, which would compel the recalcitrant witness to immediately accompany him back to Newport. He obtained the writ late in the day and planned to serve it early the next day. When he went to a local stables the next morning for a horse and buggy, the same clergyman was already there.

The deputy demanded service—he was, after all, on official business. The clergyman balked—he had been there first. No doubt wanting to get rid of both of them as soon as possible, the stableboy had two horses and two buggies brought around and was happy to see them go. The deputy and the minister left on a desperate steeplechase through the countryside for Mrs. B.'s house.

Howland had the faster horse and soon outpaced his opponent. With the witness's house in sight, he made the mistake of stopping for a moment at a blacksmith, requesting the man to accompany him and aid in serving the writ. Perhaps he was expecting further trouble and thought having a burly blacksmith with him would help. While waiting for the smith, the minister's buggy raced by in a cloud of dust.

The minister ran into a neighboring house, and a moment later a woman ran out of the back door, across the fields and into Mrs. B.'s house.

When the vexed Howland arrived a few minutes later, perhaps unsurprisingly, he found that Mrs. B. was at death's door. Her condition had only worsened since last night, and he was warned that it "would be as much as the woman's life was worth to remove her."

A sympathetic doctor was called in to confirm the diagnosis offered by the concerned family and friends, and a defeated Howland returned to Newport without her.

The defense would also raise the possibility of a conspiracy being afoot. For them, however, Sarah Cornell had conspired with others to have her revenge upon Ephraim Avery—that her pregnancy (by another man, of course) and suicide were all parts of a plan to discredit him.

The jail where Avery spent four months of his life is now an inn, the interior décor of which acknowledges the building's history. *Photo by Robert O'Brien.*

Two weeks into the trial, alone in his cell and fighting a creeping sense of hopelessness, Avery had a revelation. He later wrote:

> *After a tedious day in court, I returned to my cell. I sat down to meditate and reflect—my mind was not sufficiently calm, my thought too much scattered, and my anxiety for the result of the trial too great. Under these circumstances, I betook myself to prayer about 11 o'clock at night, at the foot of my couch. I lifted my soul to God in fervent supplication for his blessing, and determined to continue until God should be pleased, in his infinite mercy, to send relief to my soul. While thus wrestling with God in prayer, I experienced such a manifestation of the divine goodness as I never before felt. My anxiety was gone, all was sweet submission to the will of God, and from that moment I became perfectly satisfied that all would, in some way, work for the glory of God. From that time to the close of the trial I was freed from that anxiety which I had too much indulged.*

Avery was certainly not the first man to find God in a jail cell, but he is among the more articulate. If nothing else, it may have given him the strength to ignore the groups who frequently gathered under his window to taunt him.

About the same time, the publication ban imposed by Justice Eddy was broken when the editor of the *Boston Morning Post* began running the reports supplied by his reporter, Thomas Gill Jr.

This annoyed Eddy, who reprimanded the reporter and grudgingly lifted the ban. The floodgates opened, and other newspapers began publishing the transcripts their reporters were sending in. Interest in the case ran so high that court transcripts ran on the front page of some newspapers, such as the *Fall River Recorder*, at a time when news began on page two. The story would be carried in newspapers from Maine to as far south as Georgia and as far west as Ohio.

CHAPTER 12

"BEYOND ALL REASONABLE DOUBT"

T he defense opened its case on the afternoon of Thursday, May 16. Mason assigned his trusted lieutenant Richard Randolph to make the opening statement.

"Never in the course of my life have I risen in a Court of Justice under feelings so deeply painful as those by which I am now oppressed," he intoned. After promising to keep his emotions in check, he warned, "I never saw a jury placed in such a situation where they were so able to do wrong with the most honest intention of doing right."

Placing his faith in the jury's impartiality, he then stated, "Our first point is that *no* fact testified to in this case goes to prove that the death of Sarah Cornell was *not* a suicide."

Avery's Newport trial was really the defense team's show. The prosecution had made its case solidly and succinctly, illustrating the major points, and now the defense, taking the stage, built its case forcefully and thoroughly. Over the next two weeks, members of the defense would call witnesses to counter the prosecution's version of events to create reasonable doubt in the jury's minds—"Beyond all reasonable doubt, Mr. Attorney himself will tell you," Randolph said, referring to Attorney General Greene. "But gentlemen, it is your reason which is to be satisfied, not his."

The defense began by disputing Wilbur and Hooper's estimation that Sarah was about four-and-a-half-months pregnant at the time of her death. She was, they insisted, much further along that that. In fact, she was probably already pregnant at the Thompson camp meeting, and Avery could certainly not be the father of her child.

Dismissing Wilbur and Hooper's opinions, which were based on the size and development of the fetus, Randolph declared, "I think we will satisfy you that the children of women of bad fame, of deceased women, and those who indulge in promiscuous intercourse are smaller than the children of other women."

To that end, half a dozen doctors were called to dispute the prosecution's claims. Wilbur and Hooper were far too young and inexperienced to accurately judge the fetus's age by its size and weight. Clearly, they had failed to take into account the mother's moral character—and the effect it would have on the development of her child.

What of Lucretia Rawson's testimony that "she was unwell as women are once a month" before the Thompson camp meeting but not after it?

Dr. Walter Channing, professor of midwifery and medical jurisprudence at Harvard College, coolly observed, "Women of loose habits are more irregular, I believe, in their monthly discharges, than are virtuous women." The others agreed that while it was uncommon, it was certainly possible for a woman to be "unwell" even when pregnant.

The bruising that Wilbur and Hooper thought indicated violence was merely the blood settling lower down in the body as it hung suspended, the doctors insisted. This was commonly seen in suicide by hanging. Not knowing the difference between bruising and livor mortis was a mark of youthful inexperience, it was said.

While one of the doctors was giving his lengthy medical testimony, a deputy sheriff, described as "somewhat advanced in years," fell asleep in his chair. A nearby attorney, noticing the dozing deputy, tapped him on the shoulder. The man bolted to his feet, calling, "Order, gentlemen! Order!"

The entire courtroom burst into loud laughter. Justice Eddy smiled, nodded and the deputy slowly took his seat.

Reverend Henry Mayo (seemingly no relation to the family that had sheltered the fleeing Avery in New Hampshire) had attended the Thompson camp meeting and noticed Sarah. "There was something peculiar in her walk," he said. "Her clothes did not appear to be large enough—they did not come together behind." (Sarah was probably wearing a kind of long, fancy blouse over a simple gown. We might assume that being "extremely fond of dress," even on a mill girl's modest salary, she wore something like her "Sunday best" at the meeting. The more expensive, puffy-sleeved blouses laced up the back, and this is probably what Mayo refers to.)

As Sarah went by, he remarked to his wife that "she ought to be married to save her credit."

Chief Justice Eddy asked for clarification. "Do you mean she had the appearance of being pregnant?"

"Yes, sir."

Greene rose to his feet for cross-examination, "What was there in her walk?"

"She walked different from the other ladies."

"How?" Greene asked. "Describe it."

"It was something irregular, not such a gait as young ladies usually use."

"How was it different? Longer or shorter, or wider or how?"

"Some were longer and some shorter. It was irregular. I don't know as I can describe how it was."

"How wide was the opening?"

"About half an inch," Mayo said. "Principally, the opening of her clothes attracted my attention."

"How was her size?"

"I don't recollect that she looked any larger than the others," Mayo admitted.

Patty Bacon, another Thompson attendee, had pointed Sarah out to a "sister Waters" and asked what woman that was.

"That is no married woman," sister Waters replied haughtily. "She is a girl."

"She is a married woman…or she ought to be," Patty said meaningfully.

"When she went into the inner tent and changed her dress," Patty now testified before the court, "I looked over to see her when she had her dress off, and my opinion was—"

"We don't want your opinion," Greene objected. "Tell what you saw."

"Her countenance—her appearance—," Patty stammered.

"What do you mean by the countenance?" Justice Eddy inquired.

"I mean her countenance looked as though she was in a state of pregnancy…her countenance was sickly and looked like a person in the state I have mentioned."

"What was the appearance of her bosom?" Randolph asked.

Now Patty probably felt the three men were ganging up on her. She did her best to answer the various questions put to her, even as Randolph repeatedly asked for a description of Sarah's bosom. One begins to wonder if this was for the benefit of the case or of the lawyer. Patty described Sarah as sickly and pale, and when she removed her green spectacles her "eyes looked as if she were not well."

"Do you feel authorized to draw the conclusion from a pale countenance and dull eyes and not feeling well that such was her situation?" Greene demanded.

"I have told you all I have got to say," Patty said in a small voice.

As at the Bristol hearing, Sarah's character and sanity were remorselessly attacked. This case serves as an early example of the art of character assassination in court.

Dr. William Graves, the Lowell physician who had diagnosed Sarah with "the foul disease" and who later, according to her, had made improper advances, was called to testify.

"When she first came in she appeared very modest and appeared well," Dr. Graves said. "All at once she began to talk in a strange way. I began to incline to suspect she was partially insane."

Asenath Brown, who had worked with Sarah as a weaver in the Waltham Factory in Massachusetts a few years before, said that "she manifested a strange appearance. I have seen her start suddenly from her work as if something had alarmed her. She would go limping along as if afraid some one was in pursuit of her."

She further stated that one day in the mill, Sarah left her loom and went into an empty room and shut the door behind her. She had a length of cord in one hand. After a few moments, Asenath, concerned for her erratic workmate, followed. She found Sarah, cord in hand, "looking up, as if for something to hitch it to."

Sarah startled as Asenath opened the door, guiltily hid the string in her skirts and dashed from the room.

"I did believe Maria would make away with herself," Asenath said.

Another woman who had known Sarah, Elizabeth Shumway, stated that they were once sitting in a window together looking out over the water, and Sarah said how pleasant it was to see it...and that she wished herself at the bottom of it.

"But why?" Elizabeth had asked.

"I was disappointed in marriage—a man named Grindall Rawson courted me and my sister got him away from me by art and stratagem, and he married her. But," Sarah added with a sly smile, "I have one thing to comfort me."

"What is that?" Elizabeth asked.

"He likes me best—he has owned it to me, and my sister is jealous, because we have been as intimate as husband and wife," Sarah whispered.

According to Sarah, Grindall had written a poem on the flyleaf of her Bible. Strangely, Elizabeth had committed it to memory and was able to recite it to the court. It was moralizing and sentimental and read like anything but a passionate love poem, with verses such as:

> *Will you, my friend, this trivial deem—*
> *This simple offering of esteem,*
> *Accept it as a tribute due*
> *To youth, to friendship, and to you.*
>
> *Be careful dear in choice of friends,*
> *Take not the first that Fortune sends*
> *Until you with scrutiny and care*
> *You find the character he wear.*

And so on for a few more stanzas. If nothing else, this shows that Rawson did care for her in some way, if not romantically, and had some concerns over her choice of friends and her ability to judge character.

According to Philena Holmes, who had worked with Sarah in the Rhode Island mill village of Slatersville, she had attempted to take her own life there. Distraught over the loss of Grindall Rawson and burning for revenge against her sister, Sarah went out to drown herself. "And she was prevented by a man who followed her and hallooed to her, and gave her good advice never to do so again."

Several more witnesses were called to tell some variation of this story. With Sarah's suicidal tendencies established—at least to the satisfaction of the defense—Mason and his team went back over the stories of theft that had been brought up at the Bristol hearing. When Greene objected, the defense explained that "on the question of suicide, the moral history of the individual was a proper subject of inquiry."

Acting on this reasoning, they also rehashed the stories of her promiscuity and general bad behavior that had been heard before. The jury was titillated by tales of Sarah's escapades with various (unnamed) young men and her fondness for cherry rum.

Randolph called one Zilpha Bruce and asked, "What was her [Sarah's] character for chastity?"

"Her character was not good, she was tattling."

"But what was her character for chastity?"

"She was a young woman, unstable in her ways."

Chief Justice Eddy interposed. "Don't you know what chastity means?"

"I don't know what you mean," Zilpha said uncomfortably. "Express your meaning."

"Was her reputation that of keeping company with loose young men?" Randolph asked.

"Yes, it was," Zilpha nodded.

Ezra ("a queer tall old man") and his wife Ruhana Parker kept a tavern in Connecticut and were called upon to tell a bizarre story. Some seven or eight years before, on a snowy day in March or April, a very pregnant Sarah Cornell called at their establishment. "She looked eight or nine months gone," Ezra said.

Sarah was soon joined by one William Taylor, and they spoke together in a small room off the dining room. Mrs. Parker made them leave the door open: "We did not allow young people alone in a room together." Sarah told William that he was the father, and the shaken William denied it. She "threatened to swear a child on him" in court. They spoke late into the night and seemed to come to some sort of agreement, as William signed a paper and gave Sarah a sum of money.

Later that night, Ruhana testified, "I went up and saw her undress when she went to bed, and she had a largish blanket wrapped round her body before and behind. When she took it off, I saw nothing that looked like having a child."

"When she came down in the morning, she looked as spare as any woman," her husband agreed.

It had simply been a ploy to extort money from William.

The infirm Betsey Hills made her way to the stand, walking on a pair of crutches. She was Mrs. Avery's niece, who occasionally lived with the family. In Lowell, she said, a tearful Sarah had visited, "pretending penitence," and asking to be received back into the church. The minister dismissed her. Betsey seemed troubled by the fact that Sarah did not take her bonnet off during these visits.

She also described Avery's "habit to ramble about in the places and towns where he has lived and been...sometimes walking, sometimes riding; he would be out from morning till dark." So the long "ramble" around Aquidneck Island was not out of character, and a number of other witnesses had already testified to the mild weather on the day in question.

Betsey lived with the family in Bristol until September, when she moved to Connecticut.

It was the pink letter that instructed "when you write direct your letter to Betsey Hills Bristol and not as you have to me." That letter was dated November, at which point Betsey was no longer in Bristol. Avery maintained a box at the post office and picked his letters up from there; it would have been easy for him to pick out any letters from Sarah before anyone in the house saw the mail, and postal records would not show him receiving mail addressed to him from Fall River.

Sarah supposedly had expressed a deep bitterness toward the Methodist Church in general and Avery in particular.

Ellen Griggs, described as a "young married woman," and Miriam Libby, "a young woman," each testified that Sarah told them at different times of her resentment toward Avery and that she "would be revenged on him if it cost her life."

Lucy B. Howe said that Sarah came to her after being read out of the Lowell church and asked her to sign a certificate, forgiving her sins. According to Lucy, Sarah said, "The time will come when Mr. Avery and all the Methodists will repent of it. I will be revenged upon him if it costs my life."

"She said it with a look that frightened me," Lucy said. "I thought her a poor creature, and that she must be deranged."

The character assassination wasn't only practiced upon Sarah. Certain witnesses and their testimony had to be disputed.

Jane Gifford once again testified that Avery told her he was visiting with "Brother Cook" on the island, but not a single islander named Cook had seen him on December 20, nor expected to see him. As before, a number of witnesses were called to impugn her character.

As one such witness, described as "a young fellow," left the stand, Jane's long-suffering father, "his stern features exhibiting extreme impatience and anger," could stand no more.

"I wish they would ask this witness what Jane Gifford has done, to make these people try to ruin her!" he shouted.

"You must keep still Mr. Gifford," said Greene, holding up a cautioning hand. "I will take care of that."

"I can't keep still. She is my *darter*—I must speak."

"Then you had better go out, Mr. Gifford."

"Well, I will go out. I can't stand it here."

Gifford stomped toward the door. The witness who had just defamed the old man's daughter in open court reached the exit at the same time. Gifford glared at the fellow and raised "his brawny arm, as if to annihilate him," when several friends approached and asked him to calm down.

"Well, well—I won't hurt him," Gifford said grudgingly, and he left the courtroom.

Sarah Jones, much to her chagrin, found herself once again called by the defense to tell her story of seeing a man pass her house near the coal mines on December 20. When she again insisted that she had seen the man in the late morning and not the early afternoon, Mason went on the attack, accusing her of changing her testimony. Nathaniel Bullock, who had questioned her at Avery's as he chalked out a map on the kitchen floor, said that "she testified at Bristol that she was pretty positive it was between 11 and 12 o'clock. I was surprised, because she said at Avery's her impression was that it was somewhere around three o'clock."

The defense went so far as to produce a neighbor, William Simmons, to swear that Sarah had told him at the time that she had seen the man in the afternoon.

Sarah Jones had recently moved to Fall River and taken a mill job. The defense now paid her way to Newport and lodged her in a boardinghouse with their other witnesses. She was immediately made to feel unwelcome. She reported that she was harassed by the others, who confronted her with accusations of lying in court. Things became so bad that she switched boardinghouses halfway through the trial without telling the defense she had done so.

Much was made of the knot that had been tied around Sarah Cornell's neck. The prosecution argued that a clove hitch was more of a sailor's knot and would have been unfamiliar to a mill girl. The defense responded by putting a series of mill girls on the stand to testify that they used clove hitch knots on their looms. But according to Sarah Jones, before she changed her lodgings, those very same women were sequestered in a room of the boardinghouse and spent much of the night practicing tying clove hitch knots. One, Louisa Whitney, who had also been at the Thompson camp meeting, was having an especially hard time with the knot, and asked for Sarah Jones's help.

"I never saw one made in my life," Louisa said hopelessly.

Yet a few days later, Louisa swore that she used clove hitch knots to mend the harness of her loom.

"When I found one of those very girls came forward in court and swore she had been used to seeing it in making harnesses, and showing her it might have been used by the deceased to hang herself," Sarah Jones said after the trial, "I then regretted extremely I had not told that this very girl had been drilling to practice that maneuver all the evening, and that they did not, when I was with them, appear to understand how to make it, and asked me to show them."

One day during the trial, a Reverend Griffen tiptoed over to Jeremiah Mason and said, "Mr. Mason, Mr. Mason! I have a most important matter to communicate. The Archangel Gabriel came to my bedside during the slumber of the night and told me that brother Avery is innocent!"

Without so much as looking up from what he was doing, Mason grumbled, "Then let him be subpoenaed immediately."

Griffen slunk away.

The prosecution had called Margaret Hambly and Gardener Coit to testify to a tall man in a cap having visited their tavern in Fall River on December 20. The public and the prosecution were both certain that this was Avery, waiting to keep the fatal meeting with Sarah. Greene asked the waitress and the barkeep to make an identification. Margaret had proved laughably unable to pick out Avery at the Bristol hearing and was now more straightforward in her uncertainty. Coit's identification was half-hearted at best. Both had mentioned a peddler being present; Mason found the man, Isaac Alden, and had him brought to court. Alden testified to seeing and even eating with a tall man wearing a cap but said simply, "The prisoner is not the man I took tea with."

Peleg Cranston, keeper of the stone toll bridge that connected Aquidneck Island to Tiverton, also had his testimony questioned.

Reverend Daniel Webb and his driver, Benjamin Tilley, crossed the bridge in a carriage on January 19. Avery had been acquitted at the Bristol hearing and now was missing. Naturally, he was the subject of small talk throughout the region. While making change for the men in their carriage, Webb alleged that Cranston said it was all a sad affair and added that as far as he knew, Avery could not have crossed the bridge that day.

"Why didn't you say so at Bristol?" he was questioned.

But Cranston only repeated that Avery could not have crossed the bridge, and Webb and Tilley drove on.

David Davol was a local blacksmith who lived on the island and had been working in Tiverton for a few weeks in December. On the night of December 20, he returned across the bridge and, finding the gate locked, jumped down onto the beach and walked around. The tracks that Cranston noted the next morning were his and not the fleeing Avery's, returning to the island under cover of darkness.

Davol further testified that Cranston had met Avery on two occasions— "He said he should have known him if he passed."

What must have made all this especially awkward is the fact that Peleg Cranston's son, Henry, was a member of Avery's legal team. We can only imagine what it was like for the son to sit by and watch while his father's testimony was attacked and he was all but called a liar.

A number of witnesses were now called to account for Avery's movements at the Thompson camp meeting on Thursday, the day of his assignation with Sarah, according to Grindall Rawson. Reconstructing his day was intended to establish an alibi for the time he was supposed to be meeting Sarah in the wood beyond the campground.

Reverend Mayo, the same man who had particularly noticed the gap in Sarah's clothing, was with Avery for much of that day. In fact, they were together when the horn blew for preaching—the signal to meet Sarah. Mayo and Avery were together from the sounding of the horn until about nine o'clock at night. "He could not have been out of my sight for more than three minutes at a time in all that time," Mayo insisted.

Several others followed suit. In his summation, Mason would later recap their testimony:

There is, perhaps, no point of evidence of a more critical nature, than an alibi. *It is so laid down in the books, and it is always difficult to prove; but be it what it may, it is here proved, unless the witnesses are perjured. The meeting in the woods must have taken place, if at all, at the time when we show that the defendant was in another place. Whether the horn blew at half past 7, or not, is immaterial. That was the signal agreed upon for the assignation. Now eight witnesses testify that he was at that time in the Weston tent, and two testify they saw him the whole evening. Take the facts, as proved, and the story of the deceased must be false.*

The letters still remained a stumbling block for the defense. They had been admitted and read to the jury, and remained strong evidence in the prosecution's favor. How best to explain them away?

Eldridge Pratt was another traveling salesman, who had been in Iram Smith's store for about two hours one day when a tall man wearing a cap and cloak entered. The man in the cloak went behind the counter and over to Iram Smith, who was himself sitting near where the paper was kept; the ream of white paper was close by. Pratt said the man seemed to whisper to Smith and then went out again. Within forty-five minutes, Pratt said, Harvey Harden arrived in the store and discovered the half-sheet of paper in that very ream.

On cross-examination, Greene asked, "Well, did he or did he not put a half sheet of paper into the middle of the ream?"

Pratt said he did not see him do so.

"Could you have seen him?"

"I could if I was looking out. I should think he was there long enough to do it."

On the day when John Orswell met the stranger on the dock and hesitatingly accepted the letter and ninepence, Reverend Avery was in Providence at a four-day meeting. He stayed with a Pardon Jillson and on that morning went to a sunrise prayer meeting, which ended about eight o'clock. Before he left, Reverend Jotham Horton asked him to open another prayer meeting at nine o'clock; Horton had an errand to run that would keep him from doing it himself, and Avery agreed. He then went back to Jillson's house for breakfast and then to Reverend Fuller's home, where another minister, Holoway, was staying. He arrived at Fuller's about 8:40 a.m. Holoway lived in Warren, the next town over from Bristol, and Avery was hoping for a ride home at the close of the meeting in another couple of days. He and Holoway discussed some Bible verses while Holoway shaved, and Avery took his leave to go start the nine o'clock meeting.

Horton ran his errand—picking up some books from a recently arrived sloop at the docks—and made it to the prayer meeting a few minutes past nine o'clock. The meeting had not started and Avery was nowhere in sight. Horton got things underway, and Avery suddenly appeared and stayed through the entire meeting.

Based on this account of his movements, the defense insisted that Avery had a sufficient alibi and had no time to race the admittedly short distance down to the docks and hand Orswell the letter. The prosecution felt differently—that after he parted company with Holoway, he might have had just enough time to make it to the *King Philip* and back, especially since he arrived late to the nine o'clock meeting that he promised to open.

CHAPTER 13

"WHAT SAY YOU, MR. FOREMAN?"

The summations offered by the prosecution and defense would easily fill a book the size of the one you are now holding. In fact, Hallett did publish *The Arguments of Counsel in the Close of the Trial of Rev. Ephraim K. Avery for the Murder of Sarah M. Cornell*, which runs over ninety pages of tiny print. In an age of high-flown language, the arguments have an eloquence and a force seldom seen today, as each side highlighted its strengths and glossed over its deficiencies.

Mason began by congratulating the jury on sitting through weeks of grueling testimony, saying, "A trial more extraordinary we shall not find recorded in the annals of this country." He went on:

> *How are you to dispose of the mass of testimony which has accumulated before you? The first point which is incumbent upon the government to prove in this case is that the deceased came to her death by homicide, not suicide…you must have the crime proved before you seek the criminal. What has been the testimony to this point? Not that of any person who swears he saw the mortal blow inflicted, but a mere web of trivial and in themselves unconnected circumstances woven by the skill of the prosecution into a texture of injurious probability.*

"That a girl whose character was so utterly repulsive that she could not long retain a cover for her infamy…should at length have rid herself of an existence she no longer values," was one explanation he offered for her death.

Mason checked off his criticisms of the prosecution's case—Sarah was unstable, suicidal, hellbent on revenge against Avery for reading her out of the Lowell church. The pencil note proved nothing, the knot was not a clove hitch and such a public place as Durfee's stack yard is perfect for a suicide but not for murder. No one could positively identify Avery as being anywhere near Tiverton on the twentieth and he had an alibi for the time when he was supposed to be handing Orswell the letter and the ninepence and also for when he was supposed to be keeping his tryst with Sarah at the Thompson camp meeting. He hinted that a conspiracy was afoot but failed to elaborate much further upon the idea.

All of this, he felt, created reasonable doubt that a crime had even occurred, let alone that his client, Reverend Ephraim K. Avery, was the guilty party.

He spoke for nearly eight hours. He even stopped for lunch.

Attorney General Greene's remarks were no less impassioned.

"In every case there is an abstract possibility of the innocence of the accused," he said, "but justice and truth prohibit our being led away by whimsical theories of possible innocence when no reasonable doubt of a criminal's guilt remain."

He retraced the prosecution's case, going over Wilbur's testimony that Sarah intended to have her baby and do the best she could, the evidence of the letters written back and forth and the inferences that could be drawn from them and the implausibility of her supposed elaborate plot to have her revenge via her own suicide:

> *Now, gentlemen, if the prisoner is not the perpetrator of this crime, on whom can the slightest suspicion fall on whom after this can suspicion rest for any earthly crime? I have proved beyond all reasonable doubt that he alone is the author of this deed, and I now demand of him as it is my duty to do, to account, if he can, for the death of this citizen upon the principal of his innocence. He was the last being seen in her company, and this was on the evening and near the place of her death. I demand of him to account for her. What occurred between them there, and what was the progress of her sufferings can now be known only to Him by whom nothing is unknown. The prisoner, if we may extend our charity so far as to suppose it, might not have met her there with murder in his heart, but might have been suddenly induced to take her life by the dreadful state in which his cruel attempts at producing abortion by violence may have*

left her; and to this he was doubtless impelled by the strongest motives which could influence a guilty mind trembling under the fear of detection, infamy, and ruin. Yet still I call him to account for her death upon the theory of his innocence.

Greene spoke for nearly six hours.

Chief Justice Eddy delivered a brief charge to the jury, instructing them upon some points of evidence and then reminding them that they had two questions before them: Was Sarah's death a suicide or a homicide? If homicide, was Avery the murderer?

Court adjourned about seven o'clock on the evening of Saturday, June 1, 1833. The members of the jury began their deliberations.

On Sunday morning, a few minutes before noon, a bell rung ominously, signaling that the jury had reached a verdict.

A massive crowd thronged the courtroom, spilling down the outside steps and surrounding the building. Despite the size of the crowd, pressing together and straining to hear, Richard Adams Locke wrote that "during this period of painful suspense, a silence as of the tomb pervaded the whole assembly."

Avery did his best to maintain his composure, but his hand trembled as he raised it to his forehead, and "his lips exhibited the same kind of convulsive motion which they had shown on several occasions during the progress of the trial."

The jury filed in and Avery slowly rose to face them.

The clerk of the court asked, "Gentlemen of the Jury, have you agreed upon your verdict?"

The jurors indicated that they had.

"Who shall speak for you?"

"Our foreman."

The clerk turned to the foreman, Eleazar Trevett.

"Mr. Foreman, what say you, is the prisoner at the bar, guilty or not guilty?"

"Not guilty," Trevett announced.

"Gentlemen of the Jury, as your foreman has said, so do you all say?"

"We do."

"Gentlemen of the Jury, hearken to your verdict, as the Court have recorded it. You say the prisoner is not guilty. Is that your verdict?"

"It is."

It might be supposed that chaos erupted at this point, but all was strangely calm. Richard Randolph immediately moved that the defendant be discharged. Greene made no objection.

Eddy's gavel echoed in the courtroom as the then longest trial in American history came to a close.

Avery shakily bowed to the jury and took his seat, stunned. He removed his glasses; he was weeping and probably deaf to the congratulations being offered to him and his team. He was escorted out of the courtroom and boarded a private schooner that brought him back to Bristol.

His wife, who had remained so silent during the whole ordeal and was now bouncing on her knee an infant born during her husband's imprisonment, saw him approaching their home and fell to the floor in a faint.

CHAPTER 14

"WHAT'S TO BE DONE WITH PUBLIC OPINION?"

A very took the pulpit the following Sunday to deliver a sermon before a huge crowd gathered in his modest church. Many were regular members of the congregation, but many more were simply curious to get a look at the man around whom so much suspicion and controversy still swirled.

In June, he was in Boston for the New England Conference, an annual meeting of Methodist Church officials. A tribunal was convened there to examine his case and soon issued its own verdict:

1. Resolved, By the New England Conference of the Methodist Episcopal Church, That in their opinion, the verdict of NOT GUILTY, given in favor of E.K. Avery, in the late prosecution for a capital offence, ought to be confirmed in this ecclesiastical tribunal.

2. Resolved, That Ephraim K. Avery is innocent, in the opinion of this Conference, of any criminal intercourse with Sarah M. Cornell, and of any other act, connected with this unhappy affair, at all involving his Christian or ministerial character. Therefore,

3. Resolved, That E.K. Avery's character pass this Conference in good standing, and that he be continued, in his ecclesiastical privileges and ministerial office.

4. Resolved, That in view of brother Avery's confinement and afflictions, and the influence they have had upon his health and constitution, the Bishop is hereby respectfully requested, to give him such an appointment and relation to the church, as will afford him the most favorable opportunity of recovering his health.

His health—or at least his safety—remained a matter of some concern. According to the *Boston Transcript*, he ran into trouble when at the conference:

> *The Rev. Ephraim K. Avery, having occasion to transact some business in Kilby Street on Thursday, was followed by a crowd of men, who collected round the store he had entered, using harsh and menacing language. A gentleman (a member of the Methodist church) whose store is in the same street, hearing the fact, went to the place where Avery was, offered him protection, and conducted him to his own store. Whilst passing through the street, they were assailed with opprobrious epithets and after entering the store, the crowd became so numerous (four or five hundred) that fears were entertained of personal violence. Fortunately, Sheriff Parkham happened to be in the vicinity, and exerting the prerogative of his office, dispersed the mob, and remained with Mr. Avery until a carriage was procured, and he was sent to his residence in safety.*
>
> *The Boston Centinel remarks: "the facts stated are indicative that the general sentiment of the public in this vicinity are unfavorable toward Mr. Avery. Whether that public sentiment is correct or not, will probably forever remain enveloped in the same mystery that has thus far attended the whole affair connected with the death of Sarah M. Cornell. With the trial, however, so fresh before the community, and to every body's hands, the true friends of Mr. Avery would act most prudently, by advising him to avoid unnecessary publicity, until the excitement which may exist against him, shall have subsided."*

Back home, he was hanged in effigy several times in both Bristol and Fall River. The Fall River effigy hung for over a month before it was finally torn down and dragged through the dusty streets. A coffin with his name on it was left on the lawn of his house. Anonymous broadsides depicting the murder and Avery's subsequent condemnation to Hell were published and distributed in New York and Boston.

Ballads were also written, casting recriminations in verse. "The Death of Sarah M. Cornell," sold wholesale and retail in Boston's Faneuil Hall, described Sarah's end:

> *Alas, her fatal hour had come,*
> *Her hour of tribulation:*
> *And sable evening now had spread*

Avery goes to Hell in an anonymous broadside published after the trial: "A Minister Extraordinary Taking Passage & Bound on a Foreign Mission to the Court of His Satanic Majesty!" *Courtesy Library of Congress.*

"A Very Bad Man," another anonymous depiction of the murder. Bizarre Bosch-like figures comment: "How will it be managed if it should go to a jury?" and "A jury, ye young fools, is nothing—what's to be done with public opinion?" and "I never sleep on such occasions!" *Courtesy Library of Congress.*

Its mantel o'er creation.
He says fair maid now learn your doom,
I'll ne'er convey you further,
But in this lonesome dreary place,
I quickly you will murder.

She struggling hard in life's defence,
For mercy loud was crying,
While he the cursed clovehitch knot
Around her neck was tying.
Their vile unlawful intercourse,
Unlawful fruit producing,
For which he in the stackyard hung
The girl of his seducing.

"The Clove Hitch Knot," sung to the tune of "Auld Lang Syne," had no doubt of Avery's inspiration for the deed:

'Tis said he preaches night and day,
The Devil helped him
To preach, and likewise for to pray:
What a wicked wretch he's been.

How could he stand to preach and pray
With murder in his heart?
The Devil help'd him day by day,
And he will make him smart.

"Lines Written on the death of Sarah M. Cornell" was illustrated with a coffin below the title, described the events of the case and seemed to assume the voice of Sarah herself toward the end:

Ye maidens all, both old and young,
Trust not to men's false flattering tongue;
To know a man, pray know his life:
How few there are who deserve a wife.

Though doomed I am to awful end
I ask the prayers of every friend,

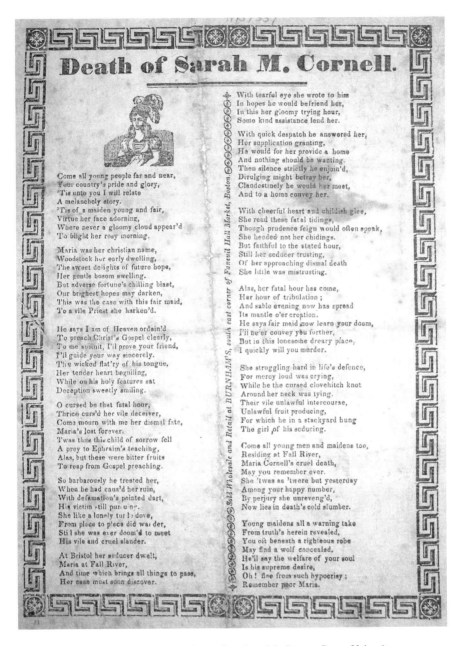

One of several anonymous poems written after the trial. *Courtesy Brown University.*

"The Clove-Hitch Knot" was sung to the tune of "Auld Lang Syne," while "The Factory Maid" was sung to "The Star-Spangled Banner." *Courtesy Brown University.*

That my poor spirit may be blest
And with my God in Heaven rest.

Now to conclude this mournful song,
These lines, I pray, remember long:
Adieu! My friends—pray don't repine;
Example's yours; experience mine.

Aside from the various ballads and broadsides, a raft of books were written about the case. Staples and Drury each published their transcripts of the Bristol hearing, and after the trial, reporters Hallett, Hildreth and Locke published theirs. In 1833, a slim book entitled *Explanation of the Circumstances Connected with the Death of Sarah Maria Cornell, by Rev. Ephraim K. Avery* appeared, allegedly Avery's confession. The story followed one popular theory of the crime—that Avery did not deliberately intend to murder Sarah, but when trying to induce an abortion "she fell to the ground a corpse!"

Avery lost no time in denying any connection with the book, writing a letter to the editor of the *Boston Transcript*, later reprinted in the *Newport Mercury* for February 8, 1833:

To The Public:
Having seen it announced that a pamphlet has been published by William S. Clarke of Providence, purporting to be the production of Ephraim K. Avery, I wish to inform the public that it is a gross imposition—I have no concern with Wm. S. Clarke or his pamphlet—The only statement I have written on the circumstances whereby I became involved in the late criminal prosecution, will shortly by published by Mr. D.H. Ela, of Boston, in connection with a vindication of my trial. Editors who have given publicity to the notice above mentioned are requested to insert this contradiction—
E.K. Avery

He soon released his version of events in *A Vindication of the Result of the Trial of Ephraim K. Avery*, as well as his own reporter's transcript with the breathless title *The Correct, Full and Impartial Report of the Trial of Rev. Ephraim K. Avery, Before the Supreme Judicial Court of the State of Rhode Island at Newport, May 6, 1833, for the Murder of Sarah M. Cornell.*

Catherine Williams, a Rhode Island author who married and quickly divorced a descendant of the state's founder, Roger Williams, hurriedly penned *Fall River: An Authentic Narrative.* Her book is very much the *In Cold*

LINES
WRITTEN ON THE DEATH OF
Sarah M. Cornell.

In lines like those, when murderers roam,
And search around for prey,
'Tis a fearful step to leave our home
Lest dangerous men betray.

This lovely girl in youthful pride
From virtue's path did stray,
A vile seducer for her guide,
And by him led away.

O, little thought the simple girl
Lured by a villain's smile,
That he from virtue's height could hurl
Her down a stream most vile.

She listened to his artful tongue,
And thought his words were true ;
Till Avery from her bosom wrung
What she did after rue.

He forced her to confess a flame,
Which his foul breath had fanned ;
And then, to her eternal shame,
Confessed his love was sham.

Love it was not, but hellish lust,
That urged this monster dire ;
On Sarah's head his passion burst,
More fierce that flames of fire.

How could she believe this murderous tale,
She knew he would deceive ;
That all his promises were frail—
He left a wife to grieve.

His infant children stretched their hands,
Beseeching her to shun
His base, unhallowed, wicked hands,
Yet still to him she run.

The voice of Heaven was heard around,
The clouds departed from above,
The evening showers had wet the ground,
But she must meet her love.

An inward warning voice alarmed,
And to her conscience spoke ;
Still the virtuous girl, unharmed,
Sought nothing to invoke.

She rushed to where her betrayer strayed,
Yet dreaming still of ill ;
She found him there, and soon 'twas said,
'Twas Heaven's, just Heaven's will.

Her lovely locks with rage he tore,
And strewed the ground with hair,
Then to a stack her form he bore,
And hung the body there.

Cold was the night, and lone the scene,
No friendly aid was nigh,
With Sarah's fate to intervene,
Or heed her dying sigh.

She's gone in regions far away,
Beyond this world of gloom,
To wait until that awful day,
When man receives his doom.

The wretch has fled from mortal's doom,
Who done this deed most vile ;
But One above can pierce the gloom,
And bring to light his guile.

Ye girls all 'round in virgin bloom,
With youth and beauty blest ;
Beware the crime, for fear the doom,
Of Sarah Maria pierce your breast.

SECOND PART.
Kind Christians all, I pray attend
To these few lines which I have penned,
While I relate the murderous fate
That did await poor Cornell's end.

Miss Sarah Cornell was her name,
Who by deceit was brought to shame ;
Your hearts in sympathy must bleed,
When shepherd's murder lambs indeed.

A Reverend Mr. Avery, sure,
A preacher of the Gospel pure,
Stands charged with murder to the test,
Seduction too, in part confessed.

First inquest he was set at large
By circumstance from further charge ;
Soon after that the deed was done—
He ran away the law to shun.

But blond for blood aloud doth cry ;
All murderers surely ought to die ;
Five hundred dollars of reward
To bring this Avery to the charge.

He soon was taken, and with speed
Was brought to answer for this deed ;
Now in Rhode Island bound was he,
In May to receive his destiny.

Me thought I heard a spirit say,
"Remember Cornell's end I pray."
And let no one reflections make
Upon my friend for my poor sake.

Let woman's weakness plead my cause,
When cruel men break nature's laws ;
If men by man was so deceived
Whni tongue would not his mercy plead.

Know you but half the awful way
That base betrayer led me astray,
The best may slip, be cautious all ;
Depraved is man since Adam's fall.

Ye maidens all, both old and young,
Trust not to men's false, flattering tongue ;
To know a man, pray know his life ;
How few there are deserve a wife.

Though shunned I am to awful end
I ask the prayers of every friend,
That my poor spirit may be blest,
And with my God in Heaven to rest.

Now to conclude this mournful song,
These lines, I pray, remember long ;
Adieu ! my friends—pray don't repine ;
Example's yours ; experience mine.

"Lines Written on the Death of Sarah M. Cornell," another lengthy ballad. Note the coffin shape at the top. *Courtesy Brown University.*

Blood of the Cornell case, as Williams interviewed many of the principals and did thorough research and theorizing to present a readable version of the story to the public. Like most other books published in the wake of the trial, it is fiercely polemic, attacking Avery and the Methodist Church and lamenting that Sarah may not have been killed had she not given in to "that baneful disposition to rove, to keep moving from place to place, which has been the ruin of so many."

Writing under the pen name Aristides, borrowed from an Athenian statesman known as "The Just," Boston clergyman and editor Jacob Frieze unloosed a tirade in a series of withering newspaper articles that were later reprinted as *Strictures on the Case of Ephraim K. Avery.* He was one of Avery's most venomous and implacable foes, for whom anything negative about the accused was obviously right and anything positive said about him undoubtedly wrong.

In more recent years, the case has served as a basis for two novels, *Avery's Knot,* by Mary Cable, and *The Tragedy at Tiverton* by Raymond Paul. Paul's version deviates considerably though entertainingly from fact.

CHAPTER 15

"REMEMBER THE STACK-YARD!"

Some weeks after the trial, Nathan Spencer, a shoemaker from East Greenwich, claimed that the previous November, when on his way into Providence, he met a man in a cloak. The young stranger asked Spencer to bring a letter to the engineer of the *King Philip* and request its delivery. The man gave Spencer some money for his trouble.

So, he claimed, it had not been Avery who handed Orswell the pink letter, but he himself.

But when he couldn't say how much money the stranger had given him, couldn't describe the letter and didn't even recognize Orswell when they eventually met face to face, everyone did their best to forget about him altogether.

By now, with books being published and even a pair of heavy-handed melodramas about the case playing on New York stages, Avery had become a liability to the Methodist Church. Whenever he preached, there was the danger of more people showing up to catch a glimpse of the man who got away with murder than were there to hear his message. When he tried preaching in Lowell shortly after his acquittal—a risky venture, considering the large number of mill girls living there—he was met with an angry crowd who hastily assembled effigies of Avery and Sarah standing by a haystack in the middle of town.

He was quietly reassigned to Richmond, Massachusetts. When his tenure there was over, he did not ask for another assignment. The church was probably just as happy. He quietly resigned the next year, saving them the embarrassment of having to expel him, and took a job as a carpenter. Avery later headed west, settling in Ohio to take up farming.

Long after Avery's acquittal, passions ran high wherever his name was mentioned.

In 1836, the twenty-six-year-old P.T. Barnum, flush with his early success with the circus, purchased a new black suit when visiting Annapolis, Maryland. His business partner, Aaron Turner, shook his head at the strutting Barnum and decided to play a joke. In a barroom, Turner observed to a group of rough-looking men, "I think it very singular you permit that rascal to march your streets in open day. It wouldn't be allowed in Rhode Island, and I suppose that is the reason the black-coated scoundrel has come down this way."

"Why, who is he?" they asked.

"Don't you know? Why that is the Rev. E.K. Avery, the murderer of Miss Cornell!"

"Is it possible?" The men flooded out of the barroom after Barnum, calling him "the lecherous old hypocrite!" "the sanctified murderer!" and even "the black-coated villain!"

Drawing near to the unaware Barnum, some shouted "Lynch the scoundrel!" while others suggested "Let's tar and feather him!"

One man grabbed Barnum by the collar while half a dozen more tore up a nearby fence, procuring a rail—the men were going to ride him out of town in a rail. Not just a strange saying, this was a bizarre and dangerous punishment where the offender was made to straddle a rail that was then hoisted up on the shoulders of several strong men who headed for the edge of town, with the offender holding on for dear life.

Barnum pleaded with the crowd, begging to be told what he was supposed to have done, and was met with "Come, straddle the rail, and *remember the stack-yard!*"

"Come, make him straddle the rail; we'll show him how to hang poor factory girls!" shouted a man in the crowd.

The man who had first collared Barnum now shouted, "Come, *Mr. Avery,* it's no use, you see, we know you, and we'll give you a touch of lynch law, and start you for home again!"

It was another few tense moments before the showman realized what was going on.

"Gentlemen! I am not Avery; I despise that villain as much as you can. My name is Barnum—I belong to the circus which arrived here last night, and I am sure old Turner, my partner, has hoaxed you with this ridiculous story."

Turner came forward and said he must have been mistaken.

"My dear Mr. Barnum," he laughed, "it was all for our good. Remember, all we need to insure success is notoriety. You will see that this will be noised all about town as a trick played by one of the circus managers upon the other, and our pavilion will be crammed to-morrow night."

It was a long time before Barnum forgave his partner for playing such a dangerous joke.

In 1838, a traveling exhibit of life-sized wax figures depicting murders and their victims, with a few infamous pirates thrown in for good measure, made a tour through the Northeast. Nathaniel Hawthorne visited on July 13, noting that among the characters on display were "E.K. Avery and Cornell,—the former a figure in black, leaning on the back of a chair, in the attitude of a clergyman about to pray; an ugly devil, said to be a good likeness." He did not describe Sarah, being more taken with the "very pretty" figure of Ellen Jewett, a New York prostitute whose murder by one of her johns was another cause célèbre. He went on to comment, "The showman is careful to call his exhibition the 'Statuary.' He walks to and fro before the figures, talking of the history of the persons, the moral lessons to be drawn therefrom, and especially of the excellence of the wax-work. He has for sale printed histories of the personages."

Some have suggested that Hawthorne may have drawn on Sarah's story for inspiration when writing *The Scarlet Letter*, but it seems to be a stretch.

A Boston newspaper wrote of the juxtaposition: "Any person who wishes to contrast triumphant vice with betrayed innocence will have an excellent opportunity by observing the countenances of Miss Ellen Jewett and Sarah Maria Cornell, which are here placed in close proximity."

Some years after it was all over, someone asked Jeremiah Mason if he really thought Avery was innocent.

Mason smiled and said, "Upon my word, I never thought of it in that light before."

In 1909, Sarah's remains were moved to a quiet section of Oak Grove Cemetery in Fall River, marked by a simple stone, much worn with the passage of time. *Photo by Robert O'Brien.*

Avery died in Pittsfield, Ohio, on October 23, 1869.

Sarah's body rested on John Durfee's farm for years, until he moved it to an unmarked location; he had grown weary of the many, many visitors to the site, knocking on his door and asking questions. In 1909, long after the border between Tiverton and Fall River had been moved and Durfee's farm became part of Massachusetts (it is Kennedy Park today), Sarah was moved to Oak Grove Cemetery, a stately garden cemetery at which a number of Fall River notables, including Lizzie Borden and her father and stepmother, her alleged victims, are also interred.

Her stone is a simple white granite, much worn with the passage of time, the words still just discernable:

In
Memory of Sarah Maria Cornell
Daughter of
James and Lucretia
Cornell
Who Died Dec 20, 1832
In the 31st Year
Of Her Age

Closing Arguments

By now, I flatter myself that the reader may be wondering, "So, Rory, what do you make of all this?"

For me, this story is part murder mystery, part human tragedy. In doing the research, I have tried to pay close attention to the words and deeds of those on the scene in 1832 and after; what those people said and did is, for me, far more interesting and illuminating than rounding up the usual class-gender-culture suspects so favored by modern theorists. This is not to say that those factors may not have some influence, but they are at best secondary considerations. In discussing this case with those unfamiliar with it, I was surprised at how many rolled their eyes and said that Avery was acquitted because a man would never be convicted of murdering a woman. While that's a quick and convenient explanation that might satisfy some, it ignores the intricacies of what really happened.

In her lifetime, and after her death, Sarah Cornell was both condemned as a whore and idealized as a poor, beautiful girl led astray. Neither picture is entirely accurate, of course. She may have been a little free with her affections, and she certainly made some bad choices, but the same can be said for so many of us. She's no more a vicious harlot than she is a doe-eyed innocent.

Did Ephraim K. Avery murder Sarah Maria Cornell? Much like Dr. Wilbur, I believe there is a difference in feeling certain and being able to swear definitely. I think he probably did, but if I had been on the jury, I wouldn't have been able to send him to the gallows.

I still have unanswered questions about her and her actions. Why does she seem so fixated on Ephraim K. Avery? After she is read out of the Lowell church, she keeps going back to him, writing letters and even visiting him. Certainly it would be just as easy for her to move on and forget all about him and what happened in Lowell. And why is she so focused on regaining those confessional letters she sent?

It seems clear that even as she leaves to keep that final appointment, she does not trust him. Why else leave behind the letters he had specifically asked her to bring, along with the ominous pencil note naming him "if I should be missing"? What did she think might happen? And why go if she had suspicions?

Avery seems like a very controlling individual, as well as a bully. He seems almost as fixated on her as she does on him. He manipulates by slandering and making threats against perceived opponents and having them read out of the church. When Sarah was simply one of his mill girl parishioners, he was in control. That he would later use her letters as leverage to extort sex from her is especially disturbing.

But when Sarah announced her pregnancy to him, their roles were completely reversed—now she was in control and had leverage with which to move him. For a control freak like Avery, this must have been equal parts galling and terrifying.

I don't think he intended to kill her; that he used a cord apparently taken from the nearby cart shows a decided lack of premeditation. He probably intended to induce an abortion, and when that failed, the panicked Avery saw only one way out.

Why was he acquitted? The defense managed to both put Sarah herself on trial, with stories of her unhappy history, and to bury the jury under an avalanche of witnesses, testimony, speculation, criticism and innuendo (as well as some things that may be outright fiction—personally, I find the Parkers' story of Sarah scamming William Taylor to be particularly fishy). The plan was to befuddle them into returning a verdict of not guilty, slowly wearing them down into a more pliable frame of mind. Hopefully, my readers do not feel similarly worked over at this point.

The prosecution called about 65 witnesses over the course of six days, while the defense took fifteen days and called about 145 witnesses—numbers are approximate; accounts differ, and it is difficult to get precise counts. The defense may have won the case simply because they took longer and had more witnesses.

While it must have been clear to the jury that an illicit encounter had taken place between the accused and the victim, the prosecution failed to conclusively place Avery at the stack yard on the night in question, and the jury bowed to reasonable doubt and let him go.

If nothing else, this case illustrates that the deepest mysteries are in what happens between two people. While the events of the story are fairly clear, many of the motives behind them remain shadowy. The principals took their secrets with them to the grave, and we may never fully understand what happened in that field in Tiverton on a cold December night so long ago.

BIBLIOGRAPHY

Aristides [Jacob Frieze]. *Strictures on the Case of Ephraim K. Avery, originally Published in the Republican Herald*. Providence, RI: William Simmons Jr., 1833.

Avery, Ephraim K. *The Correct, Full, and Impartial Report of the Trial of Rev. Ephraim K. Avery, Before the Supreme Judicial Court of the State of Rhode Island at Newport, May 6, 1833, for the Murder of Sarah M. Cornell*. Providence, RI: Marshall and Brown, 1833.

————. *Vindication of the Result of the Trial of Rev. Ephraim K. Avery*. Boston: Russell, Odiorne and Co., 1834.

Drury, Luke. *A Report of the Examination of Rev. Ephraim K. Avery Charged with the Murder of Sarah Maria Cornell*. N.p., 1833.

Explanation of the Circumstances Connected with the Death of Sarah Maria Cornell by Ephraim K. Avery. Providence, RI: William S. Clark, 1834.

Fall River Weekly Recorder. Edited by Noel Tripp. Fall River, MA, 1832–33.

Goodman, Matthew. *The Sun and the Moon: The Remarkable True Account of Hoaxers, Showmen, Dueling Journalists, and Lunar Man-Bats in Nineteenth-Century New York*. New York: Basic Books, 2008.

Hallett, Benjamin F. *Trial of the Rev. Mr. Avery. A Full Report of the Trial of Ephraim K. Avery Charged with the Murder of Sarah Maria Cornell Before the Supreme Court of Rhode Island*. Boston: Daily Commercial Gazette and Boston Daily Advocate, 1833.

Harnden, Harvey. *Narrative of the Apprehension in Rindge, New Hampshire, of the Rev. E.K. Avery, Charged with the Murder of Sarah Cornell, Together with the*

Proceedings of the Inhabitants of Fall River. Providence, RI: Marshall and Co., 1833.

Hildreth, Benjamin F. *A Report of the Trial of the Rev. Ephraim K. Avery Before the Supreme Judicial Court of Rhode Island on an Indictment for the Murder of Sarah Maria Cornell.* Boston: Russell, Odiorne and Co., 1833.

Kasserman, David Richard. *Fall River Outrage: Life, Murder, and Justice in Early Industrial New England.* Philadelphia: University of Pennsylvania Press, 1986.

Locke, Richard Adams. *Report of the Trial of the Rev. Ephraim K. Avery, Methodist Minister, for the Murder of Sarah Maria Cornell.* New York: William Stodart, 1833.

Newport Mercury. Edited by Williams and J.H. Barber, 1833.

Providence Daily Journal. Published by John Miller, 1833.

Providence Journal. "The Sensation of Half a Century Ago, the Murder of Sarah M. Cornell." January 11, 1885.

Staples, William R. *A Correct Report of the examination of the Rev. Ephraim K. Avery, Minister of the Methodist Church, in Bristol, Rhode Island, who was Charged with the Murder of Sarah M. Cornell.* Providence, RI: Marshall and Brown, n.d.

The Terrible Hay-Stack Murder. Life and Trial of the Rev. Ephraim K. Avery for the Murder of the Young and Beautiful Miss Sarah M. Cornell, a Factory Girl of Fall River, Mass. Philadelphia, PA: Barclay and Co., [1870s?].

Williams, Catherine R. *Fall River: An Authentic Narrative.* Edited by Patricia Caldwell. New York: Oxford University Press, 1993.

Williams, Gurdon. *Brief and Impartial Narrative of the Life of Sarah Maria Cornell.* New York: G. Williams, 1833.

ABOUT THE AUTHOR

Rory Raven is a performer who presents a mind reading show around the country. Closer to home, he is the creator and guide of the Providence Ghost Walk, the original ghosts and graveyards walking tour that runs through the haunted history of the city. He loves a good spooky story. He lives in Providence, Rhode Island, with Mrs. Raven and various animals.

Visit us at
www.historypress.net